C000244451

THE COCKTAIL WORKSHOP

In *Oats in the North, Wheat from the South,* author Regula Ysewijn acknowledges the rotten bridge between cheap and plentiful sugar and slavery in the Caribbean. This is also true for rum and its relatives, for which many of the recipes in this book call, and the early American sugar industry in colonial Louisiana. "Sugar has a cost," Ysewijn writes, "and that cost was paid by those in bondage."

Running Press
Hachette Book Group
1290 Avenue of the Americas, New York, NY 10104
www.runningpress.com
@Running_Press

Printed in China

First Edition: October 2021

Published by Running Press, an imprint of Perseus Books, LLC, a subsidiary of Hachette Book Group, Inc. The Running Press name and logo is a trademark of the Hachette Book Group.

The Hachette Speakers Bureau provides a wide range of authors for speaking events. To find out more, go to www.hachettespeakersbureau.com or call (866) 376-6591.

The publisher is not responsible for websites (or their content) that are not owned by the publisher.

Print book interior design by Amanda Richmond.

Library of Congress Control Number:2021938081

ISBNs: 978-0-7624-7297-0 (hardcover),
978-0-7624-7298-7 (ebook)

RRD-S

10 9 8 7 6 5 4 3 2 1

THE COCKTAIL WORKSHOP

AN ESSENTIAL GUIDE TO CLASSIC DRINKS AND HOW TO MAKE THEM YOUR OWN

STEVEN GRASSE & ADAM ERACE

Original Recipes by Lee Noble with Adam Erace

Running Press

PHILADELPHIA

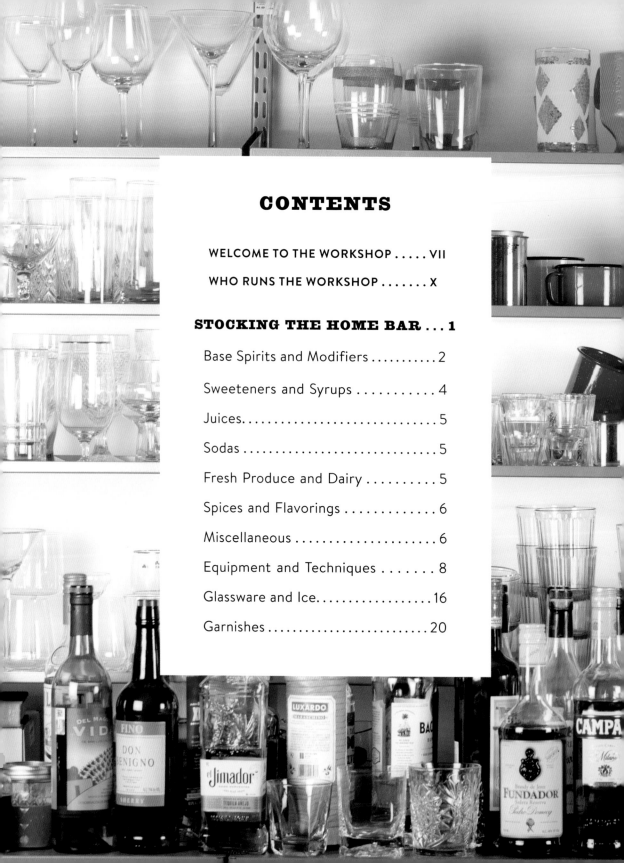

CONTENTS

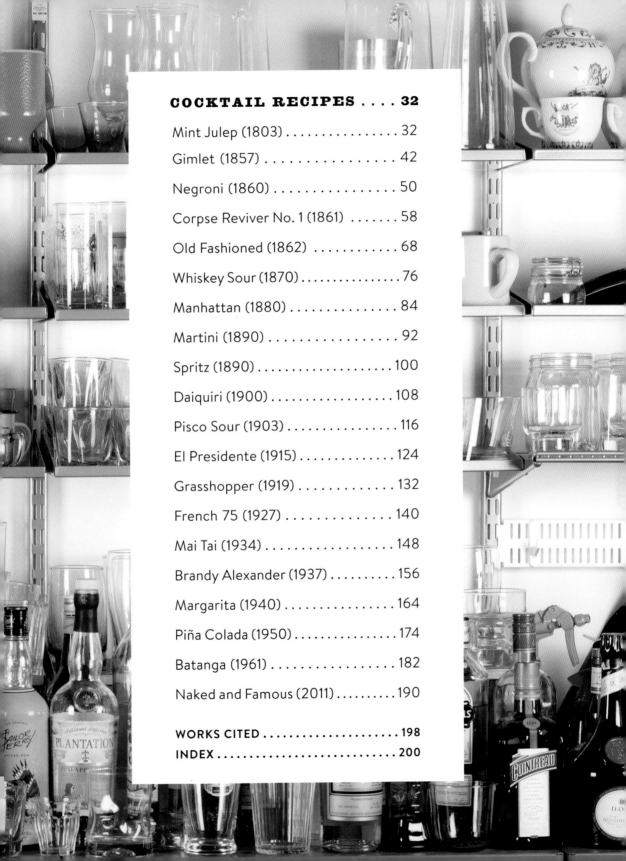

WELCOME TO THE COCKTAIL WORKSHOP!

———————◇———————

Oh, you don't know anything about mixing drinks at home? Nice. You picked up the right book.

Oh, you already know a lot about mixing drinks at home? Nice. You picked up the right book.

We're publishing *The Cocktail Workshop* with the belief that learning is a lifelong pursuit, so whether you can launch a flotilla of Mai Tais with your eyes closed or don't know the difference between tequila and mezcal, this book will help you deepen your knowledge and up your game.

Here's how the book works: We've collected the recipes, mythologies, and nerdy details of 20 classic cocktails, from the Mint Julep (page 32) to the Margarita (page 164). Each drink forms a self-contained chapter with three components—the Classic, the Riffs, and the Workshop—a liquid curriculum, if you will. The goal is to nail what makes an iconic cocktail tick, then continue along to the variations.

Think of the riffs as cousins of the classics—related but independent. Each riff section contains a suite of three drinks. Some of these interpretations are well established cocktails that are considered classics in their own rights, like the Rob Roy (page 86), kin to the Manhattan (page 84), and the Martini's (page 92) predecessor, the Martinez (page 96), but most are original cocktails developed expressly for this book. The riffs proceed up a ladder of increasing complexity. We call these ascending levels Apprentice, Journeyman, and Master, drawing from the spirit of workshops around the world and the talented craftspeople who make them hum.

The Apprentice level involves easy swaps and substitutions, such as replacing the gin in a Gimlet (page 42) with arak to create an Arak Gimlet (page 44) or using coconut water and rhum agricole to flip the frothy, creamy Piña Colada (page 174) into the Piña Arriba (page 176), a sipper befitting a dignified evening.

The Journeyman level introduces extra elements, including homemade syrups, cordials, tinctures, and infusions, which deepen the complexity of the original cocktail while also building the relationship between your bar and your kitchen. Earl Grey Syrup turns the French 75 (page 140) into the Brit 75 (page 142), for example. Mulled wine and spice-steeped brandy transform the stiff Corpse Reviver (page 58) into the autumnal Sanderson Sister sangria (page 62).

The Master level cocktails have multiple Journeyman modifiers, some of which require advance planning, plus what bartenders call an elevated serve: more intricate garnishes, specialty glassware, etc. Instead of crushed ice, the Home Stretch (page 36) arrives over watermelon granita. A hollowed pineapple carries the sized-for-two Running Mates (page 128). You won't get a diploma or pay bump for graduating to this tier, but your cocktails will be damn impressive.

The third section of each drink chapter is the Workshop. Each workshop presents a technique (Flaming Garnishes, page 195), project (Solera Aging, page 55), or DIY ingredient (Grenadine, page 129) that's germane to its classic cocktail and will lift your home mixology to a rarefied level.

The Cocktail Workshop meets you where you are. You can begin at the beginning with two- and three-ingredient bangers like the Martini (page 92) and Negroni (page 50) or cannonball into the deep end of fat-washed whiskies, fresh-fruit shrubs, and postmodern slushies. As the book's name implies, *The Cocktail Workshop* is about learning, tinkering with, and mastering a craft—the craft of mixing cocktails. Let's get to work.

WHO RUNS THE WORKSHOP?

STEVEN GRASSE,
FOUNDER, ART IN THE AGE,
TAMWORTH DISTILLERY, QUAKER
CITY MERCANTILE

Hometown: Souderton, PA

Classic Cocktail: Rye Manhattan (page 84)

The Cocktail Workshop **Crush:** Breakfast Manhattan, Reversed (page 88)

Drink When I'm Not Drinking: Bubbly seltzer water

Mixing Soundtrack: David Bowie

Cocktail Snack: Dry-roasted Planter's peanuts

Dream Bar: Tokyo's Old Imperial Bar, designed by Frank Lloyd Wright in 1923

Hangover cure: Exercise

SONIA GRASSE,
COFOUNDER,
ART IN THE AGE,
TAMWORTH DISTILLERY

Hometown: Philadelphia

Classic Cocktail: Negroni (page 50)

The Cocktail Workshop **Crush:** Rose Gimlet (page 45)

Drink When I'm Not Drinking: Structured water

Mixing Soundtrack: DJ Jake Rudh's weekly Transmission dance broadcast

Cocktail Snack: Cornichons, trashy barbecue chips, Mahina Mele macadamia nuts

Dream Bar: Chateau Marmont pool bar

Hangover cure: Federal Donuts' fried chicken sandwich

LEE NOBLE,
HEAD MIXOLOGIST,
ART IN THE AGE

Hometown: Philadelphia

Classic Cocktail: Negroni (page 50)

The Cocktail Workshop **Crush:** The Home Stretch (page 36)

Drink When I'm Not Drinking: Ginger beer with bitters and a lime wedge

Mixing Soundtrack: A Tribe Called Quest

Cocktail Snack: Ordering from the raw bar

Dream Bar: Panda and Sons, Edinburgh, Scotland

Hangover cure: Middle Child's breakfast sandwich with black coffee

ADAM ERACE,
FOOD AND TRAVEL WRITER,
COOKBOOK AUTHOR,
RETIRED BARTENDER

Hometown: Philadelphia

Classic Cocktail: Bourbon Manhattan (page 34)

The Cocktail Workshop **Crush:** 80-Proof and Sunny (page 168)

Drink When I'm Not Drinking: Pennsylvania Dutch Birch Beer

Mixing Soundtrack: Spotify "Kitchen Swagger" playlist

Cocktail Snack: Marinated Castelvetrano olives, wasabi-soy almonds, Parmigiano-Reggiano drenched in honey

Dream Bar: Lobby bar and terrace at the Grand Hotel Timeo, Taormina, Sicily

Hangover cure: Bowl of cereal before bed

DANIELA FEDOROWICZ,
PHOTOGRAPHER

Hometown: Westmoreland,
New Hampshire

Classic Cocktail: Manhattan (page 34)

The Cocktail Workshop **Crush:**
Modena Spritz (page 103)

Drink When I'm Not Drinking:
Overly caffeinated sparkling tea

Mixing Soundtrack: Tom Waits
or Ella Fitzgerald

Cocktail Snack: Cheese and
charcuterie board

Dream Bar: Just a camp mug
by the fire

Hangover cure: Flank steaks
and wet socks to bed

RON SHORT,
ILLUSTRATOR

Hometown: Burlington, New Jersey

Classic Cocktail: Coffee is my only vice

The Cocktail Workshop **Crush:** Orgeat
(page 153) with seltzer and lemon

Drink When I'm Not Drinking: Kale
smoothie

Mixing Soundtrack: My very loud
Vitamix blender, which drives everyone
in the office kitchen nuts

Cocktail Snack: Zack's Mighty Tortilla Chips

Dream Bar: Naked Lunch's counter at
Mom's Organic Market

Hangover cure: Competitive road cycling

KEVIN FLAGLER,
ART DIRECTOR

Hometown: Horsham, PA

Classic Cocktail: Old Fashioned
(page 68)

The Cocktail Workshop **Crush:**
Oaxacan Negroni (page 54)

Drink When I'm Not Drinking:
Way too much coffee

Mixing Soundtrack: Charlie
Christian with some Ella sprinkled in
and a dash of Dinah Washington

Cocktail Snack: Peanuts

Dream Bar: In the middle of the
woods, maybe it's snowing, maybe it
was designed by Richard Neutra, and
maybe I also live there

Hangover cure: Water with sea salt
and honey

Jillian Anderson, Kurt Cain-Walther,
Becca Jordahl, and other past and present
members of the Art in the Age–Tamworth
Distilling–Quaker City Mercantile team also
contributed to *The Cocktail Workshop*. This
book would also not be possible without the
bartenders, historians, and cocktail writers
whose works we reference within: M: Carrie
Allan, Dave Arnold, Talia Baiocchi, Simon
Difford, Jason Eisner, Erin DeJesus, Carey
Jones, John McCarthy, Brett Moskowitz,
Leslie Pariseau, Joaquín Simó, Robert
Simonson, and David Wondrich, among
others. Cheers!

STOCKING THE HOME BAR

One of the most daunting things about delving into a new cocktail book, especially if you don't already keep a thoroughly kitted out home bar, is the long list of products you're told you need to buy before even using the book. You can just feel your credit card melting in your wallet, right? We don't want to do that to you, which is why we've broken down everything you will need for *The Cocktail Workshop,* according to both base spirits and modifiers, as well as according to the Classic and Riff levels.

If you're starting from scratch, the first section will help you lay the foundation for a smart, functional home bar—you might even have some of the bottles kicking around already. You'll be able to mix 20 classic drinks with this basic arsenal, plus hundreds of others we only wish we had room for in these pages. You can also feel free to edit the selections as you please. We call for both Bourbon and rye, for example, but you can really use them interchangeably in any whiskey cocktail. The Spritz (page 100) calls for prosecco, while the French 75 (page 140) specifies Champagne, but if you pick one bottle of bubbles and let it do double duty, guess what? The cocktail cops aren't coming.

When you progress to the Riffs and Workshops—or if you're beginning this book from a more experienced place—it's easy to overfill a shopping cart with various expressions of gin, six types of rum, and several unusual amari. Our advice: Pick a cocktail chapter that intrigues you and build from there.

THE BASIC ARSENAL

BASE SPIRITS

Brandy, American
Calvados
Cognac
Gin, London Dry
Mezcal, joven
Pisco, Peruvian
Rum, white
Tequila, blanco
Whiskey, Bourbon
Whiskey, rye

MODIFIERS

Aperol
Campari
Chartreuse, yellow
Cointreau
Crème de cacao, dark
Crème de cacao, white
Crème de menthe, green
Curaçao, dry
Vermouth, blanc (bianco)
Vermouth, dry
Vermouth, sweet
Wine, Champagne
Wine, prosecco/cava

RIFFS AND WORKSHOPS

BASE SPIRITS

Apple Brandy, American
Armagnac
Brandy, Spanish (de Jerez)
Cachaça
Genever
Gin, Old Tom
Gin, Western Style
Mezcal, reposado
Pisco, Chilean (aged)
Rhum agricole
Rum, añejo
Rum, Navy-strength
Rum, overproof
   (Jamaican)
Rum, pineapple
Rum, spiced
Tequila, añejo
Tequila, reposado
Vodka
Whiskey, Irish
Whisky, Scotch

MODIFIERS

Absinthe
Amaro, Averna
Amaro, Braulio
Amaro, Nonino
Amaro, Vecchio del Capo
Arak
Bénédictine
Chartreuse, green
Cider, dry
Fernet-Branca Menta
Génépy
Grand Marnier
Kahlua
Lillet, blanc
Maraschino
Salers
Select aperitivo
Sherry, Fino
Velvet Falernum
Wine, Cabernet Sauvignon
Wine, Champagne rosé
Wine, Crémant
Wine, Lambrusco
Wine, Pinot Noir

SWEETENERS AND SYRUPS

Agave Syrup, light
Apple Butter
Grenadine
Lime Curd
Maple Syrup

Orange Marmalade
Orgeat
Sugar, cubes
Sugar, demerara
Sugar, granulated

SIMPLE SYRUP

MAKES ABOUT 1 CUP / 236 ML

½ cup / 118 ml water

½ cup / 100 g granulated sugar

Bring the water to a boil in a small pot over medium-high heat. Remove the pot from the heat, add the sugar, and stir to completely dissolve. Allow the finished syrup to cool. Transfer it to an airtight container or plastic squeeze bottle and store in the fridge, where it will keep for 2 weeks.

DEMERARA SYRUP

MAKES ABOUT 1 CUP / 236 ML

½ cup / 118 ml water

½ cup / 125 g demerara sugar

Bring the water to a boil in a small pot over medium-high heat. Remove the pot from the heat, add the sugar, and stir to completely dissolve. Allow the finished syrup to cool. Transfer it to an airtight container or plastic squeeze bottle and store in the fridge, where it will keep for 2 weeks.

HONEY SYRUP

MAKES ABOUT 1 CUP / 236 ML

⅓ cup / 79 ml water

½ cup / 227 g honey

Bring the water to a boil in a small pot over medium-high heat. Remove the pot from the heat, add the honey, and stir to completely dissolve. Allow the finished syrup to cool. Transfer it to an airtight container or plastic squeeze bottle and store in the fridge, where it will keep for 2 weeks.

JUICES

Apple
Cantaloupe (page 168)
Ginger
Grapefruit, Ruby Red
Lemon
Lemon, Meyer
Lime
Lime, Key

Orange
Orange, blood
Passion fruit
Pineapple
Pomegranate
Soursoup
Sugarcane
Watermelon (page 37)

SODAS

Coca-Cola, Mexican
Cola
Ginger beer

Lemon-lime
Limonata, San Pellegrino
Seltzer

FRESH PRODUCE AND DAIRY

Apples, Granny Smith
Basil leaves
Buddha's-hand citron
Cream, heavy
Eggs
Ginger
Grapes, black/red

Half-and-half
Lemon verbena sprigs
Makrut lime leaves
Milk, whole
Peppermint leaves
Rhubarb
Spearmint leaves
Turmeric

SPICES AND FLAVORINGS

Allspice, ground
Cardamom, ground
Cinnamon, ground
Cinnamon, sticks
Cloves
Cocoa powder
Hibiscus, dried
Hops, Cascade
Orange blossom water
Peppercorns, assorted

Rose petals, dried
Rose water
Saffron
Salt, kosher
Sesame seeds
Star anise
Tamarind paste
Vanilla, beans
Vanilla, extract

MISCELLANEOUS

Almond milk, unsweetened
Almonds, toasted
Apple cider vinegar
Apricots, dried
Bee pollen
Beer, IPA
Bitters, assorted
Coconut milk
Coconut oil
Coconut water
Coffee, cold-brewed
Coffee, ground

Cream of coconut
Espresso
Lactic acid, powdered
Mango, dried
Milk, sweetened condensed
Oat milk, unsweetened
Peanuts, unsalted
Rice, long-grain white
Tea, black (loose-leaf)
Tea, Chamomile (bagged)
Tea, Earl Grey (bagged)

EQUIPMENT AND TECHNIQUES

For mixing simple cocktails, there are only a few items you need:

- **BARSPOON,** for stirring
- **BOSTON SHAKER,** consisting of interlocking large and small tins, for shaken cocktails
- **FINE-MESH STRAINER,** for removing ice chips and other particles from shaken and muddled cocktails
- **HAWTHORNE OR JULEP STRAINER,** for straining stirred cocktails
- **MALLET AND ICE BAG,** for crushing ice
- **MICROPLANE GRATER,** for zesting citrus and grating spices
- **MIXING GLASS,** a beaker-like pitcher, for stirred cocktails
- **MUDDLER,** for bruising herbs, citrus, and other ingredients
- **SHARP KNIFE,** for cutting fruit and vegetables
- **VEGETABLE PEELER,** paring knife, and channel knife, for making citrus garnishes

As you progress into the upper-level cocktails and workshops, you'll also need:

- **COFFEE FILTERS**
- **CHEESECLOTH**
- **FOOD PROCESSOR**
- **GLASS BOTTLES AND JARS,** assorted
- **HANDHELD TORCH AND BUTANE LIGHTER**
- **HIGH-POWERED BLENDER**
- **ICE SHAVING MACHINE**
- **ISI CREAM WHIPPER**
- **MIXING BOWLS**
- **OAK COCKTAIL BARREL**
- **PLASTIC CONTAINERS,** assorted
- **POTS AND PANS,** assorted
- **SILICONE ICE MOLDS** (large cube, jumbo cube, sphere)
- **STRAINER**

SHAKEN COCKTAILS

You need: Boston shaker | Fine-mesh strainer

SHAKE

The initial shake contains ice.

Step 1

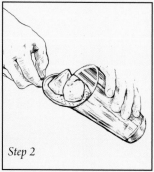

Step 2

Step 3

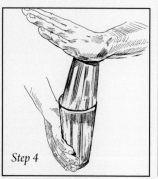

Step 4

Step 5

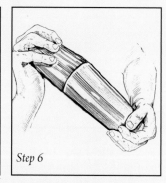

Step 6

Step 7

1. Add ingredients to the large shaker tin.

2. Fill the small shaker tin with ice.

3. Pour the ice into the large shaker.

4. Wedge the small shaker down hard inside the large one to create a tight seal.

5. Grip the shakers tightly, with the small shaker in the top hand and the large shaker in the bottom.

6. Shake back and forth from end to end for the prescribed time.

7. Strain into the glass with a fine-mesh strainer.

Examples: *Daiquiri (page 108), Margarita (page 164)*

DRY-SHAKE

The initial shake contains no ice; this is mostly used for cocktails including eggs, dairy, and other thick liquids that require extra agitation.

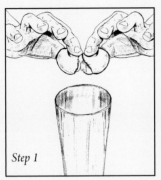

Step 1

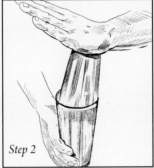

Step 2

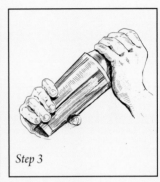

Step 3

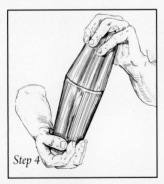

Step 4

Step 5

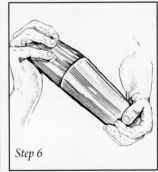

Step 6

Step 7

1. Add ingredients to the large shaker tin.

2. Wedge the small shaker tin down inside the large one to create a tight seal.

3. Grip the shakers tightly with one hand on each end.

4. Shake back and forth from end to end for the prescribed time.

5. Add ice.

6. Briefly shake to chill.

7. Strain into the glass with a fine-mesh strainer.

Examples: *Brandy Alexander Flip (page 161), Whiskey Sour (page 76)*

STIRRED COCKTAILS

You need: Mixing and/or serving glass | Barspoon | Hawthorne or julep strainer

MIXING-GLASS COCKTAILS

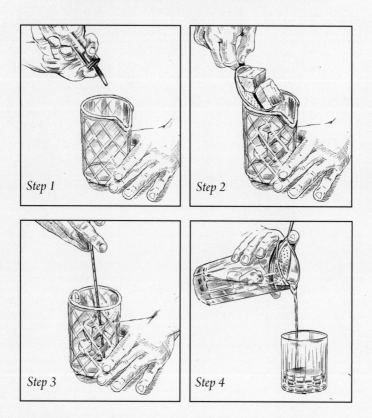

Step 1

Step 2

Step 3

Step 4

1. Add the ingredients to the mixing glass.

2. Fill the mixing glass two-thirds to three-quarters full with ice.

3. Stir briskly for the prescribed time with a barspoon.

4. Strain into the glass with a Hawthorne or julep strainer.

Examples: *Martini (page 92), Negroni (page 50)*

BUILD-IN-GLASS COCKTAILS

A simpler style of stirred cocktail.

Instead of using a mixing glass, you stir the ingredients together

in the drinking glass in which the drink will be served.

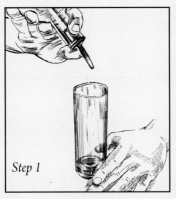

Step 1

Step 2

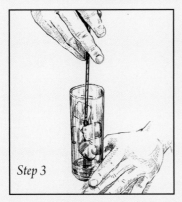

Step 3

1. Add the ingredients to the serving glass.

2. Fill the glass two-thirds full with ice.

3. Stir briskly for the prescribed time with a barspoon.

Examples: *Old Fashioned (page 68), Spritz (page 100)*

MUDDLED COCKTAILS

You need: Muddling vessel | Muddler

The process of muddling is an efficient (and therapeutic) way to extract the juices and oils from solid ingredients like herbs and fruits. The tool used to accomplish this task, called a muddler, is like an elongated pestle with a flat stopper at the bottom capable of slightly bruising or fully crushing ingredients, depending on the applied pressure—go light on the muscle in cocktails where we call for gentle muddling and firm where we call for vigorous muddling. Muddled drinks can be shaken or stirred, but the muddling always happens first.

Step 1

Step 2

Step 3

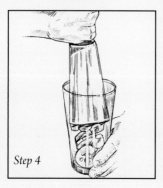

Step 4

Step 5

1. Put the ingredients to be muddled in the bottom of the vessel (serving glass, mixing glass, or shaker).

2. Grip the vessel in your non-dominant hand and the handle of the muddler in your dominant one.

3. Press the tip of the muddler down gently on the ingredients and give it a half-turn.

4. Continue to finesse the flavor out of the ingredients with a few more turns.

5. Add the liquid ingredients and ice and finish making the cocktail as prescribed.

Examples: *Garden Gimlet (page 46), Virgil's Grasshopper (page 134)*

BLENDED COCKTAILS

You need: High-powered blender

Because some drinks are just better in a blender.

Step 1

Step 2

Step 3

Step 4

1. Measure out the liquid ingredients.

2. Measure out the ice.

3. Combine them in the pitcher of the blender.

4. Blend at the designated speed for the designated time and serve.

Examples: *Running Mates (page 128), Sesamint Daiquiri (page 112)*

GLASSWARE AND ICE

FOR COCKTAILS SERVED
ON THE ROCKS (WITH ICE) OR *FROZEN*

BEER TULIP,
whose curves
emphasize foam
in Sour cocktails

COLLINS,
a taller and
narrower
highball

**DOUBLE OLD
FASHIONED,**
basically
an oversize
rocks glass

HIGHBALL,
used for fizzy
cocktails topped
with seltzer
or soda

HURRICANE,
ideal for large
frozen drinks

JULEP CUP,
traditional
pewter cup for
Mint Juleps
(page 32)

RED WINE,
for dramatic
Spritzes
(page 100)

ROCKS,
also called
a lowball or Old
Fashioned glass

SNIFTER,
which can also
be used for
up drinks

PINT,
for tiki
cocktails
containing
crushed ice
and multiple
modifiers

FOR COCKTAILS SERVED *UP* (WITHOUT ICE)

CHAMPAGNE FLUTE, for French 75s (page 140)

COUPE, also known as a Champagne saucer and an elegant vessel for any up drink

MUG, for toddies and other drink served warm

SNIFTER, which can also be used for drinks on the rocks

Occasionally in *The Cocktail Workshop,* we call for nonstandard glassware and serving vessels specific to certain drinks, such as a julep cup, hollowed pineapple, Mexican clay mug, milk and swing-top bottles, and paper snow cone cups. Substitute as you see fit.

ICE

Each cocktail served on the rocks calls for one of the ice types below, which is designated at the top of each recipe. This is your *service* ice, while your *shaking and stirring* ice should always be assumed as standard cubes.

CRUSHED, not as coarse as pebble ice but can be used interchangeably

JUMBO CUBE, the striking, slow-melting, 2 inch/5 cm cube often seen in whiskey cocktails, typically from a 6-cube silicone mold

LARGE CUBE, measuring 1¼ inches/3 cm square, typically from a 15-cube silicone mold

PEBBLE, not as fine as crushed ice but can be used interchangeably

SHAVED, essential for Margarita Raspado (page 167) but you'll need an ice shaver

SPHERE, like the jumbo cube but round

STANDARD CUBES, essentially what comes out of a plastic tray or your freezer's ice maker

GARNISHES

CITRUS

GRAPEFRUIT, LEMON, LIME, MEYER LEMON, ORANGE

EXPRESSED PEEL

Step 1

Step 2

Step 3

Step 4

1. Cut a rectangular peel about 1 inch by 2 inches/2.5 cm by 5 cm.

2. Hold it between your thumbs and forefingers over the drink with the outside of the peel facing down and pinch to release the oils.

3. Run the peel around the rim of the glass.

4. Drop the peel in the drink.

PARED PEEL

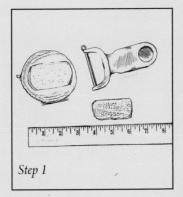

Step 1

Step 2

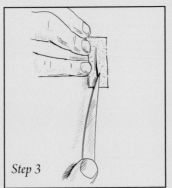

Step 3

Step 4

1. Cut a rectangular peel about 1 inch by 2 inches/2.5 cm by 5 cm.

2. Use a paring knife to trim off any rough edges and square the corners.

3. Cut a 1 inch/2 cm slit in the middle of the peel.

4. Use the slit to mount the peel on the rim of the glass with the zest facing out.

SPIRAL PEEL

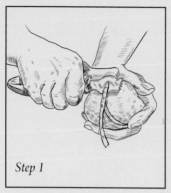

Step 1

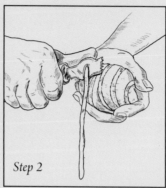

Step 2

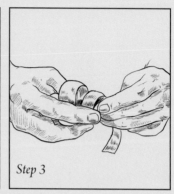

Step 3

1. Grip the fruit firmly in your nondominant hand and a channel knife in the other and start a deep crosswise cut at one end of the fruit, moving down and around.

2. Rotating the fruit as you go, slowly run a spiral pattern around it until you reach the other end.

3. Coil the spiral up in a tight spring before dropping it in the drink.

GRATED ZEST

Step 1

Step 2

Step 3

1. Hold the microplane grater in one hand over the cocktail.

2. Scrape the citrus over the holes in the grater so that the zest falls out the other side onto the surface of the drink.

3. Keep rotating the fruit as needed to find fresh skin, being mindful to avoid grating any pith.

WEDGE

Step 1

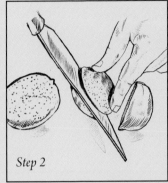

Step 2

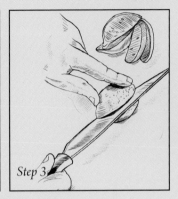

Step 3

1. Cut the fruit in half lengthwise and lay the halves flesh side down on the cutting board.

2. Cut the first one in half lengthwise, then cut into each of those sections at a 45 degree angle to make wedges.

3. Repeat for the other side of the fruit.

4. Cut a slit in the center of each wedge in order to mount to the rim of the glass.

WHEEL

Step 1

Step 2

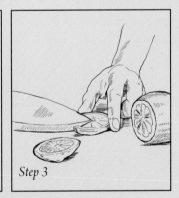

Step 3

1. Hold the fruit firmly on the cutting board and trim off the ends.

2. Slice off full cross sections of the fruit approximately ¼ inch/6 mm thick.

3. Cut a slit in from the center of each wheel in order to mount it on the rim of the glass.

SLICE

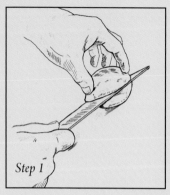
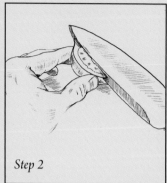

1. Cut the fruit in half lengthwise.

2. Cut a shallow slit down the middle of the flesh side from end to end.

3. Lay the halves flesh side down and slice through the fruit crosswise.

HERBS

BASIL, LEMON VERBENA, MINT, ROSEMARY, THYME

EXPRESSED

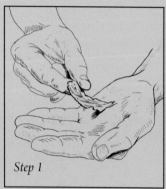

Step 1

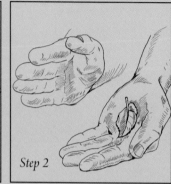

Step 2

Step 3

1. Slightly cup your nondominant hand and place the herbs in the center.

2. Cup your dominant hand the same way and clap it down over the herbs.

3. Open your hands quickly so the oils are released into the air and add the expressed herb to drink.

OTHER FRUITS AND VEGETABLES

CELERY STALKS, POMEGRANATE SEEDS, RASPBERRIES, STRAWBERRIES, PLUS THE FOLLOWING

CUCUMBER WHEEL

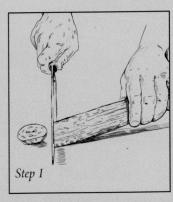

Step 1

Step 2

Step 3

Step 4

1. Trim the ends off the cucumber.

2. Slice cross sections in a wheel shape between ⅛ inch and ¼ inch/3 mm and 6 mm thick.

3. Cut a slit from the center of the wheel to the edge.

4. Use it to mount the wheel on the rim of the glass.

PINEAPPLE WEDGE

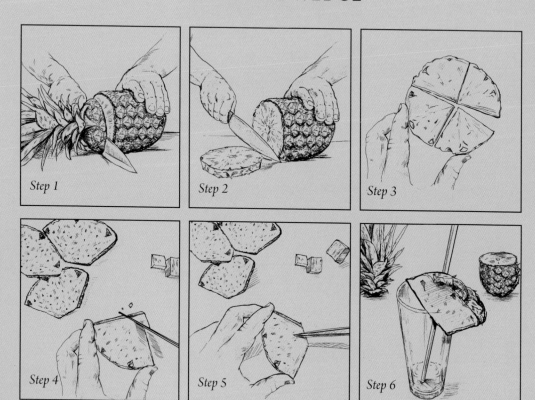

Step 1 Step 2 Step 3

Step 4 Step 5 Step 6

1. Lay the pineapple on its side on the cutting board and cut off the crown.

2. Slice off a cross section about ½ inch/13 mm thick.

3. Quarter that to make 4 wedges.

4. Cut the core off the tip of each wedge.

5. Cut a small slit in the end of the wedge.

6. Mount the wedge on the rim of the glass.

MANGO SPEAR

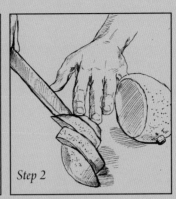

Step 1

Step 2

Step 3

Step 4

1. Slice the cheeks off the mango.

2. Slice them lengthwise into long spears about 1 inch/2.5 cm thick.

3. Carefully remove the skin by running a flexible fillet knife between the flesh and skin.

4. Tuck the spear into the drink.

WATERMELON WEDGE

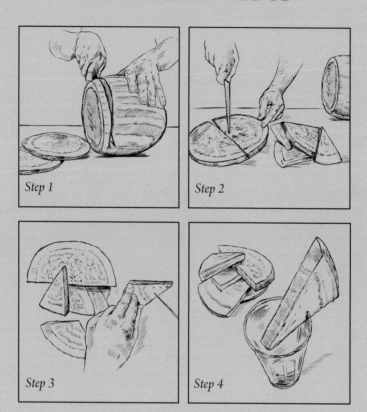

Step 1

Step 2

Step 3

Step 4

1. Cut the watermelon crosswise into wheels about ½ inch to ¾ inch/13 mm to 19 mm thick.

2. Lay a wheel on the cutting board and cut into 8 equal wedges.

3. Cut a small slit in the end of the wedge.

4. Mount the wedge on the rim of the glass.

SALT, SPICES, AND OTHER PANTRY ITEMS

Apple slices, dried
Celery seed
Chamoy
Cherries, Luxardo
Cinnamon, ground
Cinnamon, sticks
Coffee beans
Dark chocolate
Ginger, candied

Hops, Cascade
Nutmeg
Olives, green
Rose petals, dried
Salt, kosher
Salt, sea
Star anise
Straws, metal and bendy

MINT JULEP

GLASS: JULEP CUP | ICE: CRUSHED OR PEBBLE

½ ounce / 15 ml Simple Syrup
 (page 4)

8 spearmint leaves

2 ounces / 60 ml Bourbon

Garnish: Spearmint sprig

Combine the syrup and mint in a julep cup and gently muddle. Fill the cup with ice, add the Bourbon, and stir with a barspoon until the outside of the cup is frosty. Top up with more ice until it makes a mound on top of the drink. Garnish with the mint and serve.

Long before it became the official drink of the Kentucky Derby in 1938, the Mint Julep had already journeyed thousands of miles from the cradle of civilization. The origins of the word *julep* come from the Middle East, where *gulab* (Persian) or *julab* (Arabic) referred to a rose water elixir. Most cocktail historians believe this tonic spread west into Europe, losing its flowers and collecting mint along the way, and eventually crossed the Atlantic with a new name, *julep*, and an adopted home on the plantations of Virginia.

In his *Travels of Four Years and a Half in the United States of America*, John Davis retells the story of an enslaved man named Dick, who groomed the horses of a certain Squire Sutherland's rowdy son: "The first thing he did on getting out of bed was to call for a Julep; and I honestly date my own love of whiskey, from mixing and tasting my young master's Juleps." Davis included a helpful postscript, the first printed recipe for a Mint Julep: "A dram of spirituous liquor that has mint steeped in it, taken by Virginians of a morning." This was way back in 1803.

While Dick mentioned his affection for whiskey specifically, Juleps of the era were more likely to be made with "low-quality, high-proof rum (AKA 'kill-devil'). These early juleps were unpleasantly strong and skunky: room-temperature hairs-of-the-dog sucked down with a wince and a yelp," according to cocktail writer Brett Moskowitz. Finer spirits, in particular Cognac, and crushed ice replaced the cheap moonshine as the Mint Julep matured through the first half of the 1800s and maintained an association with both freed and enslaved African American bartenders. "Some of the finest examples of the early to mid-19th century were, in fact, served by proud and accomplished Black men."

One such julep maestro was Thomas Bullock, a Louisville native who mixed drinks in his hometown and at the distinguished St. Louis Country Club in the city of the same name. By the time he became the first Black bartender to author his own cocktail book, 1917's *The Ideal Bartender*, whiskey had replaced Cognac as the featured julep spirit thanks to the 1872 blight that decimated France's vineyards. Bullock's "Mint Julep—Kentucky Style" calls for Bourbon specifically and is accompanied by a sensible word of caution that still holds up: "Be careful and not bruise the Mint."

MENTA JULEP

MAKES 1 COCKTAIL

GLASS: DOUBLE OLD FASHIONED | ICE: CRUSHED OR PEBBLE

The original Mint Julep is a bright, sweet thing. Introducing Fernet-Branca Menta, the minted sister of the inky Italian amaro (and bartender favorite) Fernet-Branca, to the mix creates a bittersweet Julep you can sit with instead of slurp down. This riff doubles down on the mint, too, with both fresh muddled leaves and the persistent aroma that emerges from the bottle of Branca Menta like a green genie.

¼ ounce / 7 ml apple cider vinegar

8 large spearmint leaves

1 ounce / 30 ml Bourbon

1 ounce / 30 ml Fernet-Branca Menta

Garnish: Expressed spearmint sprig

Combine the vinegar and mint in the glass and gently muddle. Fill the glass with ice, add the Bourbon and Fernet, and stir with a barspoon until the outside of the glass is frosty. Mound more ice on top, garnish with the expressed mint, and serve.

MINT JEWEL

Want the essence of a Mint Julep without all the fuss of muddling and crushed ice? In the Mint Jewel, the classic flavors are recast in a mixed cocktail served up. Instead of fresh leaves, a spearmint syrup carries the herbal flavor through the drink, while the addition of Curaçao brings a welcome citrus note.

2 ounces / 60 ml Bourbon

½ ounce / 15 ml Spearmint Syrup

½ ounce / 15 ml dry Curaçao

Garnish: Expressed spearmint leaf

Chill the glass. Combine the ingredients with ice in a mixing glass and stir with a barspoon for 30 seconds. Strain the cocktail into the glass, float the expressed mint on the surface, and serve.

SPEARMINT SYRUP

MAKES ABOUT 1½ CUPS / 350 ML

1 cup / 236 ml water

40 large spearmint leaves

1 cup / 200 g granulated sugar

Bring the water to a boil in a small saucepot over medium-high heat. Add the mint, cover, and turn off the heat, allowing the mint to steep for 5 minutes. Skim off the leaves and press as much liquid out of them as possible into the pot. Return the pot to medium-low heat and add 1 cup sugar, stirring to completely dissolve. Remove the mixture from the heat and allow it to completely cool. Transfer the finished mint syrup to an airtight container and store in the refrigerator, where it will keep for 2 weeks.

◄ Menta Julep, Mint Jewel, The Home Stretch

THE HOME STRETCH

GLASS: DOUBLE OLD FASHIONED | ICE: WATERMELON GRANITA

Imagine a Mint Julep in which the glittering peak of crushed ice is made not with water but watermelon. Refreshing, right? A homemade watermelon granita forms the foundation of the Home Stretch, chilling down and slowly melting into a mixture of Bourbon infused with basil—we gave mint the day off—and a ginger-and-peppercorn-spiced syrup made from ultra-fragrant makrut lime leaves. You can find these leaves fresh at farmers' markets in citrus-growing areas and at groceries specializing in Southeast Asian ingredients, but dried ones, which are widely available online, work just as well.

2 ounces / 60 ml Basil Bourbon

½ ounce / 15 ml Makrut Lime Syrup

Garnish: Expressed basil sprig

Chill the glass and pack it with the watermelon ice. Combine the Bourbon and syrup in a Boston shaker with ice and vigorously shake for 10 seconds. Strain over the watermelon ice and stir with a barspoon to mix the cocktail and settle the ice. Mound more watermelon ice on top, garnish with the expressed basil, and serve.

BASIL BOURBON

MAKES 1½ CUPS / 350 ML

1½ cups / 350 ml Bourbon

20 expressed large basil leaves

Combine the ingredients in an airtight container and allow to infuse for 2 hours. Skim off the leaves and press as much liquid out of them as possible into the container. Strain the Bourbon into a clean airtight container to remove any leftover basil debris. This will keep indefinitely at room temperature, but the basil flavor will begin to degrade after 1 month.

WATERMELON GRANITA

MAKES ABOUT 16 CUBES
(1 STANDARD ICE CUBE TRAY)

1 small seedless watermelon

Cut the melon into slices, removing and discarding the rind. Process the flesh in an electric juicer. Alternately, puree the flesh in a blender and transfer the puree to a fine-mesh strainer set over a mixing bowl. Allow the juice to strain off for about 1 hour. Freeze the watermelon juice in an ice cube tray until completely solid. Remove the frozen watermelon ice and pulse in a blender until it reaches a chunky, crushed consistency. (You'll have more than you need for 1 cocktail.) Reserve in the freezer until ready for use.

MAKRUT LIME LEAF SYRUP

MAKES ABOUT 1 CUP / 236 ML

¾ cup / 177 ml water
6 fresh or dried makrut lime leaves
½ tablespoon chopped fresh ginger
½ teaspoon cracked white peppercorns
¾ cup / 150 g granulated sugar

Bring the water to a boil in a small saucepot over medium-high heat. Gently crush the leaves in your hand to release the essential oils. Add the leaves, ginger, and peppercorns and slightly decrease heat to maintain a lazy boil for 10 minutes. Turn off the heat and strain the mixture, discarding the solids and returning the liquid to the saucepot. Set it over low heat and add the sugar, stirring to completely dissolve. Remove the mixture from the heat and allow it to completely cool. Transfer the finished makrut lime syrup to an airtight container and store in the refrigerator, where it will keep for 2 weeks.

The Bourbon and the mint are lovers.
In the same land they live, on the same
food they are fostered. The mint dips its
infant leaf into the same stream that makes
the bourbon what it is. The corn grows in the
level lands through which small streams meander.
By the brook-side the mint grows. As the little
wavelets pass, they glide up to kiss the feet of the
growing mint, the mint bends to salute them.

—JOSHUA SOULE SMITH, "THE MINT JULEP,"
    LEXINGTON HERALD, 1891

WORKSHOP
CLARIFIED MILK PUNCH

Clarifying cocktails with milk goes way back to the 1700s—Ben Franklin was a fan—when booze was harsh and refrigeration was spotty. The strange-sounding technique of purposely curdling milk with an acidulated cocktail both softens substandard alcohol's edges and guards against spoilage. Neither of those issues are very pressing in drink-mixing today, but modern bartenders rarely meet an old-timey technique they don't like, and clarified milk punches began regularly appearing on cocktail menus around the early 2010s.

As the term *punch* implies, this workshop is best undertaken as a large batch. The recipe we're using to illustrate it is Mint Julep Milk Punch, which starts with a 1½ cup/350 ml mixture of Bourbon, Simple Syrup, water (to account for the dilution ice would otherwise provide), and mint. After infusing for two hours, the mint is strained out, and the cocktail is acidulated with lemon juice. When the acid in the batched Julep encounters scalded milk, the dairy ostensibly spoils. Curds form, and the impurities latch on to them like a life raft. (This is similar to how a chef clarifies a consommé, only they use egg whites instead of dairy.) After you strain the curdled concoction, you're left with a beautiful, clear punch that retains the silky texture of dairy but appears to contain no dairy at all—a milk ghost, if you will.

Once strained, bottled, and chilled, the clarified milk punch is ready to serve, but will also keep indefinitely in the fridge. While we're running the Mint Julep through the workshop, the technique will work with most cocktails that contain acid. Scale up a Margarita (page 164), Daiquiri (page 108), or Naked and Famous (page 190) by four, then proceed to the curdling stage and follow the rest of the recipe outlined below.

MINT JULEP MILK PUNCH

ACTIVE TIME: 20 MINUTES | **TOTAL PROJECT TIME:** 28 HOURS

**MAKES 4 TO 5
(3 OUNCE/90 ML) COCKTAILS**

GLASS: ROCKS | ICE: JUMBO CUBE

1 cup / 236 ml Bourbon

2 ounces / 60 ml Simple Syrup
(page 4)

2 ounces / 60 ml water

30 mint leaves, coarsely chopped

2 ounces / 60 ml lemon juice

1 cup / 236 ml whole milk

Garnish: Expressed large
spearmint leaf x 4

Equipment: 1 quart/1 L airtight
container x 4, fine-mesh strainer,
saucepot, heat-safe pitcher,
plastic wrap, coffee filters

Step 1

Start by making a batched Mint Julep.
Combine the Bourbon, syrup, water,
and mint in an airtight container and
vigorously shake for 30 seconds. Rest
the mixture for 2 hours at room temperature. Filter the mixture through a
fine-mesh strainer, discarding the solids and reserving the finished batched
cocktail.

Combine the batched Julep and
lemon in an airtight container. Shake to
integrate and set aside at room temperature. Bring the milk to a boil in a
saucepot over medium-high heat and
transfer to a heat-safe pitcher. Add the
acidulated julep to the milk, which will
curdle. Gently stir the mixture once,
careful not to break up the curds, then
swirl a few times to maximize contact
between the dairy and acidulated julep.
Cover the pitcher with plastic wrap and
allow it to rest at room temperature for
1 hour, after which the curds will have
significantly separated.

Filter the mixture through a coffee
filter, replacing the filter as many times
as needed to keep the liquid flowing.
Once the mixture has been completely
strained, transfer it to an airtight container and place in the refrigerator for
24 hours. Do not disturb the container
during this period, as the liquid needs
to remain very still for the rest of the
milk to successfully settle. Once this

has been achieved, the remaining milk solids will be in a relatively stable layer on the bottom of the container, with the clarified punch on top.

Slowly pour the clarified punch into another airtight container so that the milk solids remain undisturbed. Keep refrigerated.

To serve, set up the glasses with the ice. Evenly divide the Mint Julep Milk Punch between them and garnish each with an expressed mint leaf.

Step 2

Step 3

Step 4

Step 5

Step 6

Step 7

GIMLET

MAKES 1 COCKTAIL
GLASS: COUPE | ICE: NONE

2 ounces / 60 ml London Dry gin
½ ounce / 15 ml strained lime juice
½ ounce / 15 ml Simple Syrup (page 4)

Chill the glass. Combine the ingredients in a Boston shaker with ice and vigorously shake for 30 seconds. Strain the cocktail into the glass and serve.

More than a century before it became an official royal decree, members of the British navy consumed citrus to ward off scurvy on the high seas. To keep the juice from spoiling on long voyages, it was preserved with alcohol, then with sugar when a Scottish shipyard owner named Lauchlin Rose created Rose's Lime Cordial in 1857, the antecedent of the common sweetened bottled lime juice sold today. While the ordinary sailors would take their "medicine" with their daily allotment of rum, the officers would mix Rose's with gin.

Thus the Gimlet was born. Journalist Charles H. Baker described it as a "good cooler . . . without fancy fizzings" in Eastern ports of call, "starting with Bombay—down the Malabar coast to Colombo; to Penang, Singapore, Hong Kong and Shanghai," in 1939's *The Gentleman's Companion, Vol. II Exotic Drinking Book.* "The Gimlet is just as popular as our Martini here."

Like the Martini (page 92) and the oldest classic cocktails, the Gimlet is very simple to make. It follows the straightforward formula of spirit + citrus + sweetener; think of it as the British cousin of the Daiquiri (page 108). While bottled lime cordial may have been preferred by the British navy, fresh juice is king now.

The Master of every such Ship as last aforesaid shall serve or cause to be served out the Lime or Lemon Juice with Sugar . . . or other such Antiscorbutics as aforesaid to the Crew so soon as they have been at Sea for Ten Days, and during the Remainder of the Voyage, except during such Time as they are in Harbour and are there supplied with fresh Provisions; the Lime or Lemon Juice and Sugar to be served out daily at the Rate of an Ounce each per Day to each Member of the Crew, and to be mixed with a due Proportion of Water before being served out, or the other Antiscorbutics, if any, at such Times and in such Quantities as Her Majesty by Order in Council may from Time to Time direct.

—THE MERCHANT SHIPPING ACT OF 1867

ARAK GIMLET

MAKES 1 COCKTAIL

GLASS: COUPE | ICE: NONE

Arak (also spelled araq*) is an anise liqueur sipped in squares, souks, and cafés from Istanbul to Tel Aviv. Flavored with aniseed, think of it as the Levantine equivalent of Italian anisette or Greek ouzo. Arak's intense taste is polarizing for sure; if you like black licorice, you'll enjoy this Gimlet riff, which works off a one-to-one base-spirit substitution: out goes the gin, in comes the arak. The blend of cool, refreshing, minty anise and sharp, tart, floral lime really works. Can't find arak? Make your own by infusing vodka with toasted aniseed and a bit of sugar.*

2 ounces / 60 ml arak

½ ounce / 15 ml strained lime juice

½ ounce / 15 ml Simple Syrup (page 4)

Garnish: Expressed mint leaf

Chill the glass. Combine the ingredients in a Boston shaker with ice and vigorously shake for 30 seconds. Strain the cocktail into the glass. Garnish with the mint and serve.

ROSE GIMLET

MAKES 1 COCKTAIL

GLASS: COUPE | ICE: NONE

This Gimlet begins with an easy homemade flower syrup. Rose is the primary flavor, while hibiscus brings a balancing, cranberry tartness and lends a little color to the finished product. Shaken with gin and Key lime juice (a bit sweeter than regular), it produces a pale pink Gimlet that looks as good as it tastes. Serving note: Be sure to mist the glass with rose water inside and outside, which you can do with an atomizer—bar supply and kitchen stores sell them—or even an old cleaned and sanitized perfume bottle. Some of the rose water will get on your hands as you drink, and the experience becomes tactile. It's like making a cocktail 3D.

Rose water, in an atomizer or spray bottle, for misting

2 ounces / 60 ml floral gin

¾ ounce / 22 ml strained Rose Syrup

½ ounce / 15 ml strained Key lime juice

Garnish: Dried rose petals

Chill the glass, then mist the inside and outside of it with rose water. Combine the ingredients in a Boston shaker with ice and vigorously shake for 30 seconds. Strain the cocktail into the glass, garnish with a few rose petals, and serve.

ROSE SYRUP

MAKES ABOUT 1½ CUPS / 350 ML

1 cup / 236 ml water

¼ cup / 8 g dried rose petals

1½ tablespoons dried hibiscus

1 cup / 200 g granulated sugar

Bring the water to a boil in a small pot over medium-high heat. Add the flowers, cover, and remove from the heat. Steep for 5 minutes. Strain the mixture into a clean pot and add the sugar. Place over low heat and stir to dissolve. Transfer to a heat-safe lidded jar (like a canning jar) and reserve. This will keep refrigerated for 2 weeks.

◀ Arak Gimlet, Rose Gimlet, Garden Gimlet

GARDEN GIMLET

MAKES 1 COCKTAIL

GLASS: ROCKS | ICE: CRUSHED OR PEBBLE

Making cocktails is like cooking; it's all about layering flavor. The reason why you sweat onions and garlic as the first step in a pot of soup or sauce, for example, is akin to why you muddle the basil and cucumber as the first step in this cooling, curiously pickle-y, jade Gimlet. We bruise the herbs and cuke with salt—an abrasive—and lime juice—a solvent that helps fully extract the flavors from the ingredients—then layer in the gin and syrup. Remember: when muddling, soft herbs like mint and basil require less elbow grease than hard ones like rosemary and sage. The goal is to coax out those essential oils, not bash them into oblivion.

4 fresh basil leaves

2 cucumber wheels

1 pinch kosher salt

¾ ounce / 22 ml strained lime juice

2 ounces / 60 ml cucumber gin

½ ounce / 15 ml Simple Syrup (page 4)

Garnish: Cucumber wheel, celery stalk, celery seed

Combine the basil, cucumber, salt, and lime juice in a shaker and gently muddle. Add the gin, Simple Syrup, and ice and vigorously shake for 30 seconds. Pack the glass with the ice. Strain the cocktail over the ice and mound more ice on top. Garnish with a cucumber wheel, celery stalk, and sprinkling of celery seed and serve.

WORKSHOP:
OLEO-SACCHARUM

Oleo: oil. *Saccharum:* sugar. The Latin verbiage makes this versatile, viscous, flavor-charged style of cocktail syrup sound like an arcane potion—and it *is* quite old, dating back at least to the 18th century. *Saveur* touches on its history:

> As Jerry Thomas wrote in *The Bon Vivant's Companion,* first published in 1862, "To make punch of any sort in perfection, the ambrosial essence of the lemon must be extracted, by rubbing lumps of sugar on the rind (a process that has evolved over the years)." Cocktail scholar David Wondrich has traced oleo-saccharum back to 1707 and perhaps before, and in his definitive book *Punch,* states that "lemon oil adds a fragrance and a depth that marks the difference between a good Punch and a great one."

An oleo-saccharum is so easy to make: it just about makes itself. If you can peel a bunch of citrus, toss those peels with sugar, and be patient, you can get an oleo-saccharum. As the mixture sits, the essential oils weep from the zest, melting the sugar, and creating a thick, glossy, intensely fragrant citrus syrup. In terms of flavor and aroma per square inch, there is just no substitute for the oils locked inside the stippled rind of an orange, grapefruit, lemon, or lime. No juice-based syrup delivers as intense a payoff as an oleo-saccharum, and because of the weight of the oils, it does double duty by adding body to your cocktails.

Since we're talking Gimlets, we've formulated a lime oleo below, but the same base recipe works with any of the aforementioned citrus fruits. As they're all typically larger than limes, you need less of them. For one cup of sugar, eight lemons, six oranges, or four grapefruits create the right ratio of peel to sugar. You can also add an extra layer of flavor by introducing herbs and spices into the oleo mixture: toasted peppercorns, basil, dried hibiscus or rose petals, ginger.

LIME OLEO

MAKES ABOUT 2 CUPS / 470 ML

10 limes

1 cup / 200 g granulated sugar

1 cup / 236 ml water

Equipment: Vegetable peeler, large mixing bowl, plastic wrap, saucepot, strainer, 1 quart/1 L airtight container x 2

Thoroughly wash the limes. Using the vegetable peeler, carefully remove the zest in large strips, leaving behind the dry white pith. Reserve the peeled fruit for juicing (for this or other cocktails). Combine the peels and sugar in an airtight container. Stir the mixture so the sugar coats the peels evenly, cover, and allow it to rest for at least 24 hours at room temperature, or until the peels look shriveled and a viscous solution has started to form.

Bring the water to a low boil in a small saucepot over medium heat. Carefully scoop the lime mixture into the water, stirring to completely dissolve the sugar. Remove the mixture from the heat and pour it through a strainer to separate the peels from the oleo-saccharum. Completely cool, transfer to an airtight container, and store in the refrigerator, where it will keep for 2 weeks.

OLEO GIMLET

MAKES 1 COCKTAIL
GLASS: COUPE | ICE: NONE

2 ounces / 60 ml London Dry gin

1 ounce / 30 ml Lime Oleo-Saccharum

¼ ounce / 7 ml strained lime juice

Garnish: Expressed lime peel

Chill the glass. Combine the ingredients in a Boston shaker with ice and vigorously shake for 30 seconds. Strain the cocktail into the glass. Express the lime over the surface of the drink, rub it around the rim, drop it in the cocktail, and serve.

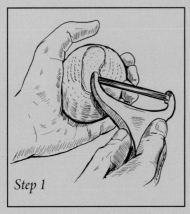

Step 1

Step 2

Step 3

Step 4

OTHER OLEO-FRIENDLY COCKTAILS

CHILCANO SOUR (page 119): Replace the Quick Ginger Syrup with an equal measure of lemon-ginger oleo-saccharum.

FRENCH 75 (page 140): Replace the Simple Syrup with an equal measure of lemon oleo-saccharum.

WISCONSIN BRANDY OLD FASHIONED (page 71): Replace the fresh orange and sugar cube with ½ ounce/15 ml orange oleo-saccharum.

NEGRONI

MAKES 1 COCKTAIL
GLASS: ROCKS | ICE: LARGE CUBE X 2

1 ounce / 30 ml gin

1 ounce / 30 ml Campari

1 ounce / 30 ml sweet vermouth

Garnish: Expressed orange peel

Combine the ingredients with ice in a mixing glass and stir with a barspoon for 15 seconds. Set up the glass with the ice. Strain the cocktail into the glass. Express the orange peel over the surface of the drink, rub it around the rim, drop it in the cocktail, and serve.

While the Negroni is considered one of the *most* classic cocktails, this amber, all-booze sipper is thought to have grown out of another drink: the Milano-Torino, a mix of Campari (made in Milan) and sweet vermouth (made in Torino) shot with seltzer and garnished with a lemon peel. During World War I, the easygoing Mi-To became popular with US servicemen stationed in Italy, where it took on the nickname it's now known by today: the Americano.

Different origin stories credit competing counts, Camillo Negroni and Pascal Negroni, with inventing the Americano riff that would eventually bear the family name. The drink's true father is debated, as is the location of its invention. Was it Camillo, who allegedly asked a bartender at Caffe Casoni in Florence to replace the seltzer in his Americano with gin sometime around 1920? Or was it Pascal, a Corsican general stationed in colonial French Senegal, who created the drink in honor of his wedding in the 1860s? Whatever the real story, the switch turned a bubbly, thirst-quenching long drink into a stiff short drink that went on to conquer modern cocktail culture.

The classic Negroni formula is equal parts gin, Campari, and sweet vermouth, but you can tinker with the recipe based on your preferences. A huge gin fan might bump up the base spirit in a 2-1-1 ratio. Someone looking for a more bitter-forward Negroni might do the same with Campari. While vermouth plays a bit of a third wheel here, you can create a lot of variation by experimenting with different types. Using rich, full-bodied Carpano Antica Formula, for example, will produce a different Negroni than French Dolin Rouge, a lighter style. Think about matching the vermouth to the gin. Piney, juniper-forward gins from the London Dry school need a vermouth that can stand up to them, while the botanical profiles of modern-style gins like Hendrick's are better matched to mellower vermouths. Experiment. Cocktails can be classic, but that doesn't mean they're carved in stone.

CIDER SBAGLIATO

MAKES 1 COCKTAIL
GLASS: RED WINE | ICE: LARGE CUBE x 4

Campari attributes the Negrino Sbagliato to Mirko Stocchetto, a bartender at Bar Basso in Milan. In 1972, Stocchetto mistakenly added prosecco instead of gin to a Negroni, a fortuitous accident that's lower in proof than a traditional Negroni but not as flitzy as a Spritz. (Sbagliato means "mistaken" in Italian.) This twist on the Sbagliato sources its bubbles from cider rather than prosecco, and you want one that's very dry. If you're unsure of a cider's sugar level, most French bottles are safe bets, though we love the "Stark" Stayman-Spitzenberg blend from our neighbors, Ploughman Cider, in Adams County, Pennsylvania.

1 ounce / 30 ml Campari

1 ounce / 30 ml sweet vermouth

**Dry cider to top, about
4 ounces / 120 ml**

Garnish: Expressed lemon peel

Set up the glass with the ice. Add the ingredients and briskly stir with a bar-spoon for 5 seconds. Express the lemon peel over the surface of the drink, run it around the rim, drop it in the cocktail, and serve.

Cider Sbagliato, White Negroni, Oaxacan Negroni ▶

WHITE NEGRONI

MAKES 1 COCKTAIL

GLASS: ROCKS | ICE: LARGE CUBE X 2

Think of the White Negroni as the classic formula's blonde younger sister. It's not actually white, but soft yellow. The color comes from Salers, a bitter oak-aged gentian aperitif, which swaps in for Campari, and nimble, aromatic Lillet Blanc, which replaces sweet vermouth. Blended with gin in the same equal-parts ratio, the result preserves most of the proof of the original Negroni, but has a layer of sweetness that brings to mind melted lemon hard candies.

1 ounce / 30 ml gin

1 ounce / 30 ml Salers gentian aperitif

1 ounce / 30 ml Lillet Blanc

Garnish: Expressed lemon peel

Combine the ingredients with ice in a mixing glass and stir with a barspoon for 15 seconds. Set up the glass with the ice. Strain the cocktail into the glass. Express the lemon peel over the surface of the drink, rub it around the rim, drop it in the cocktail, and serve.

OAXACAN NEGRONI

MAKES 1 COCKTAIL

GLASS: ROCKS | ICE: JUMBO CUBE

Imagine a Venn diagram with three circles: smoky, bitter, and sweet. The Oaxacan Negroni would live within that intersection. So would coffee, which bridges smoky mezcal, bitter Campari, and sweet vermouth in this riff. While you can certainly make your own, store-bought cold brew works well here. Just be sure to use a full-strength variety, as the more delicate flavor of a light roast will get lost.

1 ounce / 30 ml joven mezcal

1 ounce / 30 ml Campari

1 ounce / 30 ml sweet vermouth

¾ ounce / 22 ml strong cold-brew coffee

Garnish: Expressed orange peel, 6 drops cardamom bitters, such as Dashfire or Fee Bros.

Combine the ingredients with ice in a mixing glass and stir with a barspoon for 15 seconds. Set up the glass with the ice. Strain the cocktail into the glass. Express the orange peel over the surface of the drink, rub it around the rim, and drop it in the cocktail. Garnish with cardamom bitters and serve.

NEGRONI ALTERNATES

CAMPARI DRINKER'S NEGRONI

1½ ounces / 45 ml Campari

¾ ounce / 22 ml gin

¾ ounce / 22 ml sweet vermouth

GIN DRINKER'S NEGRONI

1½ ounces / 45 ml gin

¾ ounce / 22 ml Campari

¾ ounce / 22 ml sweet vermouth

WORKSHOP:
SOLERA AGING

In Jerez, Spain, the ancestral home of sherry, the famous fortified wines are aged using the solera method, a multiyear process of blending that results in each barrel containing several different ages of sherry. Think of it like sourdough bread made from a mother that's been passed down through the generations. Every new loaf contains a bit of the old.

Other fortified wines like Madeira and Lillet are made this way as well, but you can also apply the process to cocktails. The Negroni is perfect for it. Jarred and aged a month, the gin, Campari, and sweet vermouth meld into a better, more homogenous version of the cocktail you were trying to mix in the first place. This happens on a molecular level, with time and exposure to oxygen doing the work of your hands and a mixing spoon. The gin's harsh edges soften, the tannins in the vermouth and bitterness of the Campari relax, and the aged cocktail that emerges after a month is more concentrated in flavor but also a smoother drinking experience.

You could stop there and have an excellent batch of cocktails on your hands—one bottle each of gin, Campari, and sweet vermouth will yield about 24 month-aged Negronis. But you're only going to pour off half that amount for drinking, saving the rest for the next stage in your solera. Each month you'll pour off half of the last batch and add new gin, Campari, and sweet vermouth. In effect, you're layering flavors, so that within 4, 6, or twelve months, you'll have a Negroni batch comprised of 4, 6, or twelve different ages. (Once bottled, these should be stored in a cool, dark place, where they'll keep forever.) You can continue this process indefinitely, but just saying, for example, if you start in January you'll have 120 single-serve solera-ed Negroni by November. One of those and a copy of *The Cocktail Workshop* would make an excellent holiday gift.

SOLERA-AGED NEGRONI

ACTIVE TIME: 30 MINUTES | TOTAL PROJECT TIME: 1 TO 12 MONTHS

MAKES 1 STARTER BATCH

1 (750 ml) bottle gin

1 (750 ml) bottle Campari

1 (750 ml) bottle sweet vermouth

Equipment: 1 gallon/3.8 L lidded glass jar, funnel, 1 quart/1 L lidded glass jar

Combine the ingredients in the gallon jar; there should be 3 to 4 inches/8 to 10 cm of headspace. Screw on the lid and gently shake. Store in a cool dark place for 1 month. Using a funnel, pour off and bottle half the aged Negroni for consumption; it will be enough for about 12 cocktails.

To the remainder in the jar, add half a bottle (13 ounces/375 ml) each of gin, Campari, and sweet vermouth. Store in a cool dark place for 1 month. Pour and bottle half the aged Negroni, which is now a blend of 2 different batches: 1 month old and 2 months old. Continue the process, refreshing every month, for as long as desired.

To serve, pour 3 ounces/90 ml of the Solera Negroni into a rocks glass filled with 2 ice cubes. Express an orange peel over the surface of the drink, rub it around the rim, drop it in the cocktail, and serve.

Step 1

Step 2

Step 3

Step 4

OTHER COCKTAILS TO SOLERA AGE

CORPSE REVIVER №1

MAKES 1 COCKTAIL
GLASS: COUPE | ICE: NONE

1½ ounces / 45 ml Cognac

¾ ounce / 22 ml Calvados

¾ ounce / 22 ml sweet vermouth

Garnish: Expressed orange peel

Chill the glass. Combine the ingredients with ice in a mixing glass and stir with a barspoon for 30 seconds. Strain the cocktail into the prepared glass. Express the orange peel over the surface of the drink, rest it on the rim of the glass, and serve.

Great name for a cocktail, right? No one knows who came up with the catchy moniker for this amber necromancer (not to be confused with the circa-1930s Zombie), but its earliest appearance in print dates to 1861, when London's *Punch* magazine wrote of a hangman who "after liquoring up with a Sling, a Stone Wall, and a Corpse-Reviver . . . merrily danced forth into the middle of the room, and sang a little song with this agreeable refrain . . ."

Made with two types of French brandy—Cognac (made from grapes) and Calvados (made from apples)—and sweet vermouth, the Corpse Reviver No. 1 can definitely make a body dance and sing, though it's unlikely the anonymous hangman's 19th-century version contained those exact ingredients. The first published recipe, from 1871's *The Gentleman's Table Guide,* calls for brandy, Maraschino, and Boker's bitters (the leading bitters brand from the 1820s through Prohibition). We don't arrive at the established brandy-Calvados-sweet vermouth mix until 1930, when it appears in Harry Craddock's *The Savoy Cocktail Book.* Craddock distinguishes this recipe as the Corpse Reviver *No. 1.* His Corpse Reviver No. 2 is a lithe and citrusy ballet of gin, Lillet, Cointreau, and lemon with a scintilla of absinthe. They're very different drinks but could be members of the same aristocratic French family, perhaps a generation apart.

The No. 2 went on to eclipse the original in popularity, and since then bartenders have ushered new Corpse Revivers into the world. But the stiff, noble No. 1 bears the numerical distinction for a reason: it's not only a true classic but also an enduring relic from an era when brandy—until recently imprisoned at the dusty back of the bar—was a status symbol.

REANIMATOR

MAKES 1 COCKTAIL

GLASS: ROCKS | ICE: JUMBO CUBE

France isn't the only producer of fine brandies. The spirit is also made in Andalusia, Spain, where brandies age in the solera method (see page 55), just like the area's most famous liquid export of sherry. (Sherry is the anglicized word for Jerez, the Andalusian city and epicenter of sherry production.) Unlike smooth, luxurious Cognac, brandy de Jerez is fruity and wild, a dynamic player in the Reanimator. This apple-forward Corpse Reviver riff features two different expressions of the fall fruit: brandy and cider. For the former, we like Laird's, whose packaging looks like it hasn't changed in a century. For the latter, local is best if you live in an apple-growing region, and if not, Martinelli's produces an organic Honeycrisp cider that's delicious and widely available.

2 ounces / 60 ml apple cider

1½ ounces / 45 ml Spanish brandy (de Jerez)

¾ ounce / 22 ml American apple brandy

¾ ounce / 22 ml sweet vermouth

Garnish: Expressed lemon peel

Set up the glass with the ice. Combine the ingredients with ice in a mixing glass and stir with a barspoon for 30 seconds. Strain the cocktail into the glass. Express the lemon peel over the surface of the drink, rest it on the rim, and serve.

Reanimator, Sanderson Sister, Osiris Myth ▶

SANDERSON SISTER

MAKES ABOUT 2 QUARTS / 1.9 L

GLASS: RED WINE x 8-10 | ICE: NONE

The boozy Corpse Reviver and a fruit-filled goblet of sangria may not seem like they have much in common, but look a little closer: Both have brandy. Both have wine. Transforming one into the other doesn't take witchcraft, only some extra time to build in the layers of spice and fruit. It's a three-step process: melting honey and infusing vanilla into Cognac and Calvados, macerating apples and grapes in the brandy mixture, and mulling the wine. It can all be done ahead of time, so when you're serving, all you need to do is combine the components with a good stir and half-hour chill. This recipe makes enough for a crowd, so light a black candle and brew up a pitcher.

1 cup / 236 ml Calvados

1 cup / 236 ml Cognac

½ cup / 118 ml honey

2 vanilla beans, split and scraped

3 Granny Smith apples, cored, peeled and medium diced

3 cups seedless black or red grapes, halved lengthwise

4 cinnamon sticks

12 cloves

8 star anise

2 teaspoons black peppercorns

2 (750-ml) bottles light-bodied red wine, such as Pinot Noir

Garnish: Expressed rosemary sprigs x 8 to 10

Combine the Cognac, Calvados, honey, and vanilla in a medium pot over medium heat and bring to a simmer. Simmer for 10 minutes, then allow it to cool to room temperature. Once cool, add the apples and grapes to the pot, cover, and allow the fruit to macerate at room temperature for 1 hour, occasionally stirring to make sure all fruit gets in contact with the liquid. This can be done up to 1 day in advance; just be sure to transfer the mixture to the refrigerator after 1 hour.

Toast the cinnamon, cloves, star anise, and peppercorns in a large pot over low heat until fragrant, occasionally tossing, about 5 minutes. Add the wine, bring the mixture to a boil, then reduce the heat to low, and simmer for 30 minutes. Allow the mulled wine to cool to room temperature and strain it into a 2 quart/1.9 L pitcher, discarding the spices. (This can be done up to 3 days in advance.) Chill.

When the fruit has macerated for at least an hour, add the mixture to the pitcher, stir to combine, and chill for at least 30 minutes before serving. Divide the sangria between 8 to 10 wineglasses. Clap each sprig of rosemary between your palms to express the oils. Garnish the glasses with a rosemary sprig and serve.

OSIRIS MYTH

MAKES 1 COCKTAIL
GLASS: MUG | ICE: NONE

Named for the mythological Egyptian king who returned from the afterlife, the Osiris Myth recasts the Corpse Reviver into a hot toddy inspired by yansoon, the fragrant anise tea found in Egypt and other Eastern Mediterranean countries. The Corpse Reviver trio—Cognac, Calvados, sweet vermouth—carries over to this warming cocktail, though the vermouth gets a prior infusion with bee pollen in another nod to the ancient Egyptians, who associated honeybees with royalty and spirituality. The Osiris Myth also uses a tincture of baharat, a Middle Eastern spice blend that varies from country to country, souk to souk, merchant to merchant. Ours features cinnamon, cardamom, allspice, and cloves and makes this toddy a natural for hayrides and holiday festivities.

2 tablespoons aniseeds

4 star anise

6 ounces / 177 ml hot water

¾ ounce / 22 ml Cognac

¾ ounce / 22 ml Calvados

¾ ounce / 22 ml Bee Pollen Vermouth

4 drops Baharat Tincture

Garnish: Dried apple slice

Add the spices to a saucepot and lightly toast them over low heat, frequently stirring, until fragrant, about 5 minutes. Add the water, increase the heat to high, and allow the mixture to come to a boil. When it hits a boil, remove the pot from the heat, and allow the spices to steep in the water for 5 minutes. While they steep, warm a mug in the microwave for 15 seconds, then add the remaining ingredients to the mug. Strain the anise tea directly into the mug and stir three times to incorporate. Garnish the cocktail with a dried apple slice and serve.

BEE POLLEN VERMOUTH

MAKES 1¹/₂ CUPS / 350 ML

1½ cups / 350 ml Lo-Fi sweet vermouth

½ cup / 80 g bee pollen

Combine the ingredients in an airtight container and vigorously shake for 10 seconds. Allow the jar to rest at room temperature for an hour, then transfer it to the refrigerator for 24 hours. Strain out the bee pollen, reserving the infused vermouth. Strain the vermouth a second time through a coffee filter to remove any fine sediment. Be patient; you may have to gently wring out and replace the filter a few times. Transfer the finished vermouth to an airtight container and store in the refrigerator, where it will keep for 2 weeks.

BAHARAT TINCTURE

MAKES ABOUT 4 OUNCES / 120 ML

2 teaspoon ground cinnamon

2 teaspoon ground allspice

½ teaspoon ground cardamom

12 cloves, toasted and lightly crushed

4 ounces / 120 ml vodka

Combine the ingredients in an airtight container and allow them to infuse at room temperature for three days. Strain the mixture through a strainer lined with a coffee filter and transfer the finished tincture to a small eyedropper bottle. Store in a cool, dark place. This will keep indefinitely, but the spice flavor will begin to degrade after 2 months.

WORKSHOP:
BARREL AGING

Like the running "We can pickle that" *Portlandia* sketch, barrel aging everything from maple syrup to vinegar to beer to—in a bit of chicken-or-the-egg poetry—pickles, became A Thing in the 2000s. This process, by which liquids are rested in used (usually Bourbon) barrels, imparts a subtly sweet, smoky-oaky character with suggestions of vanilla, caramel, and spice. The technique is a natural for mixed drinks, and lately it's become hard to find a bar not touting its Bourbon barrel-aged Manhattan (page 84) or Negroni (page 50).

Thanks to the arrival of personal-sized barrels from brands like Bluegrass Barrel, home cocktail enthusiasts can try this method without committing to the typical 53 gallons most Bourbon barrels hold. Most of the mini barrels come in the 1 quart/1 L size, which will hold about 10 cocktails. The Corpse Reviver is well suited to barrel aging, as is any cocktail that doesn't contain any of the following: dairy, egg, fruit juice or perishable ingredients, or carbonation. The aforementioned Manhattan and Negroni are perennially popular, but also consider the Hail to the Chief (page 126), Martinez (page 96), and Easy Does It (page 70).

BARREL-AGED CORPSE REVIVER № 1

ACTIVE TIME: 5 MINUTES | TOTAL PROJECT TIME: 2 TO 4 WEEKS

MAKES 10 COCKTAILS

2 cups / 470 ml Cognac

1 cup / 236 ml Calvados

1 cup / 236 ml sweet vermouth

Equipment: 1 quart/1 L oak cocktail barrel, such as Bluegrass Barrel brand; 1 quart/1 L glass bottle; funnel

Combine the ingredients in the barrel, plug it closed, and gently agitate to mix. Allow the mixture to rest in the barrel for 2 to 4 weeks, testing the contents once a week to observe progress. When the desired intensity of flavor has been achieved, transfer the finished Barrel-Aged Corpse Reviver No. 1 from the barrel to the bottle and store in a cool, dark place, where it will keep indefinitely.

To serve, combine 3 ounces/90 ml of the Barrel-Aged Corpse Reviver No. 1 with ice in a mixing glass and stir with a barspoon for 30 seconds. Strain the cocktail into a chilled coupe. Express an orange peel over the surface of the drink, rest it on the rim, and serve. Alternately, the entire batch can be well-chilled and served straight from the bottle for a heavier, undiluted cocktail.

Step 1

Step 2

Step 3

OLD FASHIONED

MAKES 1 COCKTAIL
GLASS: ROCKS | ICE: STANDARD CUBES

¼ ounce / 7 ml water

1 granulated sugar cube

4 dashes Angostura Aromatic bitters

2 ounces / 60 ml American whiskey (choice of Bourbon or rye)

Garnish: Expressed orange peel

Add the water, sugar cube, and bitters to a rocks glass and vigorously muddle them until the sugar has completely dissolved. Fill the glass to the rim with ice and add the whiskey. Briskly stir to integrate the cocktail and top with more ice if necessary. Express the orange peel over the surface of the drink, rub it around the rim, drop it in the cocktail, and serve.

The Old Fashioned is so old, its recipe fits the earliest printed definition of a "cocktail" as an alcoholic beverage, (see page 73), as published in the grandiloquently named Hudson, New York, newspaper *The Balance, and Columbian Repository*. It takes just four ingredients to make this classic: whiskey, sugar, water, bitters—five if you count orange peel garnish. Before it was called the Old Fashioned, the mixture was known simply as the Whiskey Cocktail, according to *Difford's Guide*, but "beginning in the 1870s, bartenders, bewitched by the new liqueurs available to them, began making 'Improved' Whiskey Cocktails. . . . This led to a revolt among old-school imbibers, who began to call out for 'Old Fashioned Whiskey Cocktails.'"

If you're looking at this recipe and wondering, "Where're the oranges and cherries?" it's a fair question. Muddling fruit along with the sugar cube in the base of an Old Fashioned came into vogue during Prohibition, allegedly to mask the taste of subpar booze. This step has been largely jettisoned in the modern cocktail era, though persisting in regional variations, including the Wisconsin Brandy Old Fashioned (page 71). For the original, fruit remains relegated to the rim of the glass.

Rye and Bourbon are both acceptable, traditional bases for the Old Fashioned, so the choice is up to your preference. (This is the case in many of the cocktails calling for American whiskey in this book.) Rye will produce a spicier, sturdier drink, while Bourbon informs a smoother, sweeter one. For price and quality we recommend Rittenhouse rye for the former and Buffalo Trace or Elijah Craig for the latter.

WHISK(E)Y 101

RYE, BOURBON, AND SCOTCH are all types of whiskey produced from grains. Most whiskey made in the United States and Canada is rye, meaning produced from a grain blend that is at least 51 percent rye.

BOURBON is always produced in America—not just Kentucky, despite the state's effective marketing—and must be produced from a blend that is at least 51 percent corn, which lends its signature sweetness.

SCOTCH is always produced in Scotland from some proportion of malted barley, unmalted barley, and other grains. Typical blended Scotch contains at least 20 percent malt whisky, while celebrated single malts are made exclusively from malted barley and produced at single distilleries. Scotch whisky is typically spelled without an *e*, as is Japanese whisky, which is made in the Scottish style and has gained a cult following in the United States in recent decades.

EASY DOES IT

With nothing more than a sugar cube and splash of water standing in the way of the booze, the Old Fashioned is a potent cocktail. So what if you want an O.F. vibe but don't want to be falling over after two drinks? As the name of this riff implies, the Easy Does It won't knock you out. Replacing half the whiskey with dry Fino sherry reduces the overall ABV by about 25 percent. You can stretch out the booze even further by preparing this cocktail in a Collins or Highball glass and topping with seltzer.

1 ounce / 30 ml rye
1 ounce / 30 ml Fino sherry
4 dashes Peychaud's Bitters
Garnish: Expressed lemon peel

Combine the ingredients in the glass and fill with ice. Stir with a barspoon for 20 seconds to mix the cocktail and settle the ice. Add more ice to reach just below the rim of the glass. Express the lemon peel over the surface of the drink, rub it around the rim, drop it in the cocktail, and serve.

WISCONSIN BRANDY OLD FASHIONED

GLASS: ROCKS | ICE: STANDARD CUBES

Like the Grasshopper (page 132) and the Brandy Alexander (page 156), the Wisconsin Brandy Old Fashioned is a fixture of the Badger State's beloved supper club scene. This is like a souped-up O.F., with brandy subbing in for whiskey, muddled cherries and orange, and a burst of bubbles or sour mix to top it off. We have three suggested finishers in the recipe below, so you can adjust the overall profile to your tastes.

2 dashes Angostura Aromatic bitters

1 sugar cube

2 orange slices

2 Luxardo or Brandied Cherries (page 90)

2 ounces / 60 ml American brandy

Splash lemon-lime soda, seltzer, or sour mix (optional)

Add the bitters, sugar, and fruit to the glass and muddle until the sugar has completely dissolved. (Take care not to bruise the white pith of the orange, muddling only the flesh of the fruit.) Add the brandy and fill the glass with the ice. Stir with a barspoon for 20 seconds to mix the cocktail and settle the ice. Add more ice to reach just below the rim of the glass. If desired, top the cocktail with the lemon-lime soda (sweet finish), seltzer (dry finish), or sour mix (sour finish) and serve.

◀ Easy Does It, Wisconsin Brandy Old Fashioned, Cold Brew Old Fashioned

COLD BREW OLD FASHIONED

As long as whiskey and coffee have existed in the same place, people have been adding one to the other, from old Irish Coffee to the modern classic Revolver. This riff applies the Old Fashioned's whiskey-sugar-bitters trinity to a coffee cocktail, with both homemade liqueur (think Kahlua but creamy) and bottled cold-brew. We serve this drink on the rocks, but it would also be delicious warmed up and served in a mug topped with whipped cream.

1½ ounces / 45 ml Bourbon

1½ ounces / 45 ml strong cold-brew coffee

½ ounce / 15 ml Coffee Liqueur

2 dashes Dashfire star anise bitters

Garnish: Toasted star anise

Add ingredients to the glass and top with ice. Stir for 10 seconds so that the ice begins to settle into the liquid. Add more ice to just below the rim and stir again for 10 seconds. Garnish with the star anise and serve.

COFFEE LIQUEUR

MAKES ABOUT 1 CUP / 236 ML

4 ounces / 120 ml hot brewed coffee

2 ounces / 60 ml vodka

1 ounce / 60 ml heavy cream

½ cup / 100 g granulated sugar

1 teaspoon ground cinnamon

2 drops vanilla extract

Combine the hot coffee and sugar in a saucepot and set over low heat, gently stirring to completely dissolve. Remove the pot from the heat and allow the mixture to cool for 10 minutes before stirring in the remaining ingredients. Allow the coffee mixture to cool for 10 minutes, then transfer to an airtight container and vigorously shake to emulsify the cream and thoroughly integrate all the ingredients. Store the finished liqueur in the refrigerator, where it will keep for 2 weeks. Shake before using as the cream and cinnamon may separate.

THE COCKTAIL WORKSHOP

Cock tail, then in a stimulating liquor, composed of spirits of any kind, sugar, water and bitters . . . is supposed to be an excellent electioneering potion inasmuch as it renders the heart stout and bold, at the same time that it fuddles the head. It is said also, to be of great use to a democratic candidate: because, a person having swallowed a glass of it, is ready to swallow any thing else.

—*THE BALANCE, AND COLUMBIAN REPOSITORY*, 1806

WORKSHOP:
FAT WASHING

Infusing is a very effective way to get flavor into booze. It's how we make our Spiced Mango Rum (page 151), Basil Bourbon (page 36), Bee Pollen Vermouth (page 64), and several other flavored spirits in this book, but fat washing is another important, if lesser known, and nifty technique for the home bartender. You fat wash alcohol by combining it with, well, fat. Olive oil, brown butter, bacon grease, and ghee are all game, though in this workshop we're suggesting coconut oil, which lends a subtle coconut flavor that's surprising, yet welcome, in an Old Fashioned. Shaking the mixture emulsifies the fat into the spirit, and as they slowly re-separate in the fridge, the former flavors the latter. Fat washing also lends weight and body, making whiskey feel richer and allowing gin to glide across the tongue.

ACTIVE TIME: 5 MINUTES | TOTAL PROJECT TIME: 24 HOURS

MAKES ABOUT ³/₄ CUP / 177 ML

1 cup / 236 ml American whiskey (choice of Bourbon or rye)

1 ounce / 30 ml melted coconut oil

Equipment: 1 quart/1 L airtight container x 2, strainer, cheesecloth

FAT WASHING COMBINATIONS TO TRY:

Cachaça + almond butter in the White Lie (page 150)

Gin + olive oil in the Gimlet (page 42)

Tequila + pumpkin seed oil in El Capilla (page 185)

Combine the whiskey and coconut oil in the container, seal, and vigorously shake to emulsify. Store the mixture in the refrigerator for 24 hours, during which the fat will flavor the alcohol and eventually separate into a hardened layer at the top of the container. Carefully scoop out and discard the hardened fat, then pass the now fat-washed whiskey through a strainer lined with cheesecloth to remove any leftover pieces. Transfer to a clean airtight container and store in the refrigerator. It will keep indefinitely but the flavor will begin to degrade after 1 month.

Step 1

Step 2

Step 3

COCONUT OLD FASHIONED

MAKES 1 COCKTAIL

GLASS: ROCKS | ICE: STANDARD CUBES

2 ounces / 60 ml Coconut-Washed Whiskey

½ ounce / 15 ml Apricot Syrup

4 dashes Bittermen's Buckspice Ginger Bitters

Garnish: Expressed orange peel

Combine the ingredients with ice in the glass. Stir with a barspoon for 20 seconds to mix the cocktail and settle the ice. Add more ice to reach just below the rim of the glass. Express the orange peel over the surface of the drink, rub it around the rim, drop it in the cocktail, and serve.

APRICOT SYRUP

MAKES ABOUT 2 CUPS / 470 ML

1¼ cups / 295 ml water

¼ cup dried apricot, chopped

1 cup / 200 g granulated sugar

Bring the water to a boil in a small saucepot over medium-high heat and add the apricot. Reduce the heat to low and allow the mixture to simmer for 10 minutes. Strain off and discard the apricots and return the liquid to the pot. Add the sugar, stirring to completely dissolve. Remove the pot from the heat and allow to cool completely. Transfer the finished apricot syrup to an airtight container and store in the refrigerator, where it will keep for 2 weeks.

WHISKEY SOUR

MAKES 1 COCKTAIL

GLASS: ROCKS | ICE: STANDARD CUBES

2 ounces / 60 ml American whiskey (choice of Bourbon or rye)

1 ounce / 30 ml strained lemon juice

¾ ounce / 22 ml Simple Syrup (page 4)

Whites from 1 large egg

1 dash Angostura Aromatic bitters

Garnish: Skewered Luxardo or Bourbon Cherry (page 90)

Fill the glass with the ice. Combine the ingredients in a Boston shaker and vigorously dry-shake for 30 seconds. Add ice to the shaker and shake for 15 seconds. Strain the cocktail into the glass, lay the skewered cherry across the rim, and serve.

Like the Daisy (page 165), Flip (page 161), and Julep (page 32), the Sour represents a family of drinks rather than any one single cocktail. Essentially any drink constructed according to the formula of spirit + citrus + sweetener can claim common ancestry with this clan of tarts. The Daiquiri (page 108) is a Sour: rum + lime + sugar. The Gimlet (page 42) is a Sour: gin + lime + sugar. The Margarita (page 164) is a Tequila Sour with a modifier of orange liqueur. Unlike these drinks, the cocktails typically thought of as Sours clearly state their affiliation right in the name: the Amaretto Sour, the Midori Sour, the Pisco Sour (page 116), and of course, the most popular member of the family, the Whiskey Sour.

Though prototypes likely date back to the scurvy-battling British navy (see also, the Gimlet), written record of various Sours begin to appear in the 1850s, when Gin and Brandy Sours showed up on the menu at Mart Ackerman's Saloon in Toronto—"6¼" cents a piece—and in Jerry Thomas's 1862 book, *The Bartenders Guide*. It appears whiskey usurped brandy as the go-to Sour spirit sometime in the following decade and has stayed on top since.

The most critical piece of information for making an excellent Sour cocktail is not to use sweet-and-sour mix. That modern invention is a blight on the Sour family, resulting in too many horrible hangovers and bouts of acid reflux throughout the latter half of the 20th century. Around the new millennium, better bars went back to the old and proper way of doing things, eschewing bottled juices and mixes in favor of their fresh and natural ancestors, sour mix included. Lemon juice with Simple Syrup (page 4) is the clean, effective way to achieve a lip-smacking tang with none of the nonsense.

SON OF SOURS: THE COLLINS

If you add seltzer to a Sour and serve it in a tall glass, you have a Collins. The Tom Collins is basically a sparkling Gin Sour. Its brother John Collins is a Whiskey Sour made specifically with Bourbon. Convert your Sour to a Collins when you want something with a lower alcohol content and a little fizz. Drop the egg white when making a Collins.

NEW YORK SOUR

MAKES 1 COCKTAIL

GLASS: COUPE | ICE: NONE

Bartenders in the late 1800s would float a layer of claret, the old-timey British moniker for Bordeaux, over their Whiskey Sours. This wine-modified Sour went by various names through the decades, including the Brunswick Sour and Claret Snap, before the cocktail cognoscenti settled on the New York (sometimes Greenwich) Sour. Following the lead of seminal Manhattan bar Employees Only, our New York Sour is made with rye and egg white.

2 ounces / 60 ml rye whiskey

1 ounce / 30 ml strained lemon juice

¾ ounce / 22 ml Simple Syrup (page 4)

Whites from 1 large egg

½ ounce / 15 ml dry red wine, such as Cabernet Sauvignon

Chill the glass. Combine the rye, lemon, syrup, and egg in a Boston shaker and vigorously dry-shake for 30 seconds. Add ice to the shaker and shake for 15 seconds. Strain the cocktail into the glass. Place a barspoon upside down as close as possible to the surface of the drink. Gently pour the wine onto the barspoon; it will "float" on the surface of the drink. Serve.

RASPBERRY BOURBON SOUR

An effective way to weave another layer of flavor into a Whiskey Sour is by using an infused syrup instead of just plain old Simple Syrup. Try raspberries. They ripen alongside corn during Kentucky's high summer, making Bourbon a perfect guest to invite to this riff. Greek yogurt slides in to add background tang and body.

2 ounces / 60 ml Bourbon

¾ ounce / 22 ml Raspberry Syrup

¾ ounce / 22 ml Greek yogurt

½ ounce / 15 ml strained lemon juice

Whites from 1 large egg

Garnish: 3 drops Fee Bros. cherry bitters, 3 skewered raspberries

Fill the glass with the ice. Combine the ingredients in a Boston shaker and vigorously dry-shake for 30 seconds. Add ice to the shaker and shake for 15 seconds. Strain the cocktail into the glass. Garnish with the bitters, lay the skewered raspberries across the rim, and serve.

RASPBERRY SYRUP

1½ cups / 350 ml water

½ pint raspberries

1 cup / 200 granulated sugar

Bring the water to a boil in a small saucepot on the stove over medium heat. Add the raspberries, reduce the heat to medium-low, and cook for 10 minutes. Add sugar and stir to completely dissolve. Reduce the heat to low and allow the mixture to simmer for 5 minutes. Remove the pot from the heat and allow the mixture to cool to room temperature. Strain out and discard the raspberry seeds, reserving the finished syrup. Transfer to an airtight container and reserve in the refrigerator, where it will keep for 2 weeks.

◀ New York Sour, Raspberry Bourbon Sour, Triple Hopped Sour

TRIPLE HOPPED SOUR

MAKES 1 COCKTAIL

GLASS: BEER TULIP | ICE: STANDARD CUBES

From the Boilermaker to the Irish Car Bomb to the Dr. Pepper (a shot of amaretto plunged into a pint of Yuengling lager) served around our hometown of Philadelphia, pairing booze with beer is a long and storied tradition. This riff on the Whiskey Sour uses both brewed beer (in an IPA Syrup) as well as one of beer's key flavoring agents, hops, to infuse the Bourbon. Hops are the flowers of the hop plant and resemble young green pine cones with tightly clustered, overlapping leaves. There are dozens of varieties, but we call for the commonly used Cascade in this Whiskey Sour, which has a floral, grapefruity bitterness—hence the grapefruit juice and bitters in this drink. Some farmers sell hops fresh, but if you can't find them, any physical or online brewing supply store will have dried available.

2 ounces / 60 ml Hops Bourbon

¾ ounce / 22 ml strained Ruby Red grapefruit juice

¾ ounce / 22 ml IPA Syrup

Whites from 1 large egg

4 dashes Bittermens Hopped Grapefruit bitters

Garnish: 3 whole-flower Cascade hops

Fill the tulip glass with ice. Combine the ingredients in a Boston shaker and vigorously dry-shake for 30 seconds. Add ice to the shaker and shake again for 15 seconds to chill the liquid. Strain the cocktail into the glass, garnish with hops, and serve.

"Then may God have mercy on your soul," says I, taking a drink out of me cousin's glass. "Amen" says the Methodist, as he ordered another whisky sour.

—*WAUKESHA PLAIN DEALER*, JANUARY 1870

HOPS BOURBON

MAKES ABOUT 1¹⁄₂ CUPS /
350 ML

1½ cups / 350 ml Bourbon

½ loosely packed cup /
7 g whole-flower Cascade hops

Combine the ingredients in an airtight container and gently shake. Allow to infuse in a cool, dark place for 48 hours, gently shaking once a day. Strain out the hops, reserving the infused Bourbon. Squeeze any excess Bourbon out of the hops and strain the liquid to remove any particles. Discard the hops and combine the infused Bourbon back together in the container. This will keep indefinitely, but the hops flavor will begin to degrade after 2 months.

IPA SYRUP

MAKES 2 CUPS / 470 ML

1½ cups / 350 ml American IPA, such as Bell's Two-Hearted, at room temperature

1 cup / 200 g granulated sugar

Rapidly pour the beer into a cool saucepan so it foams up and releases some carbonation. Place the saucepan on the stove over low heat. Gradually raise the temperature to medium-low heat. (If this is done too quickly, the remaining carbonation will escape rapidly and foam will spill over the sides of your pan.) Continue to raise the heat until the beer is hot but not boiling. Add the sugar, stirring to completely dissolve. Remove the finished syrup from the heat and allow it to cool to room temperature. Transfer to an airtight container and reserve. This will keep refrigerated for 2 weeks.

WORKSHOP:
AQUAFABA

T hough the earliest Sours did not include egg white, it's become the standard procedure since the cocktail renaissance of the new millennium. This minimal inclusion adds a whole lot in both texture and appearance, and it's an easy extra that makes a cocktail at home feel like a cocktail out, so we include it in our Whiskey Sour recipe. But what if you can't/don't/won't eat eggs (raw or otherwise)? Aquafaba enters for a vegan version.

While the name sounds like a Latin American soft drink or bath gel you'd find on a crowded HomeGoods shelf, *aquafaba* is admittedly more appealing-sounding than "spent chickpea cooking water," which is exactly what it is. Like egg whites, aquafaba—by the way, the name, coined in 2015, is a portmanteau of the Spanish for "water" and "bean"—is protein-dense, which is why it also creates a cap of foam atop a cocktail when thoroughly agitated. The only difference, bartender Jason Eisner told *Bon Appétit* in 2016, is "Egg whites smell like wet dog, and chickpeas have no smell whatsoever." (This is why bitters often stain the snowy surfaces of egg-white cocktails; they mask any sulfur smell.)

Could you just open up a can of garbanzos and use the ready-made aquafaba you'd normally just dump down the drain? Of course. But as with anything else, making your own with dried chickpeas allows you to control the quality of the ingredients. And, bonus: Hummus goes great with cocktails.

ACTIVE TIME: 5 MINUTES | TOTAL PROJECT TIME: 15 HOURS

MAKES ABOUT 3 CUPS / 710 ML

1 pound / 456 g dried chickpeas

5 cups / 1.2 L water

1 teaspoon Morton's kosher salt

Equipment: Large pot, 1 quart/1 L airtight container

Rinse the chickpeas and allow them to soak overnight in a pot or bowl of cold water at room temperature. When ready to cook, bring the 5 cups of water with the salt to a boil in a large pot. Drain the soaked chickpeas and add them to the boiling water. Cover the pot and reduce the heat to low. Simmer for 2 hours. Remove the chickpeas with a strainer and reserve for a future use. Allow the cooking liquid (aquafaba) to completely cool. Transfer the aquafaba to an airtight container and store in the refrigerator, where it will keep for 2 weeks.

Foam fail? If a cocktail shaken with aquafaba is not foaming up properly, the aquafaba is too thin. You can fix this simply by further reducing. Place the aquafaba in a pot on the stove and boil rapidly until reduced by half. Completely cool before using.

Step 1

Step 2

Step 3

Step 4

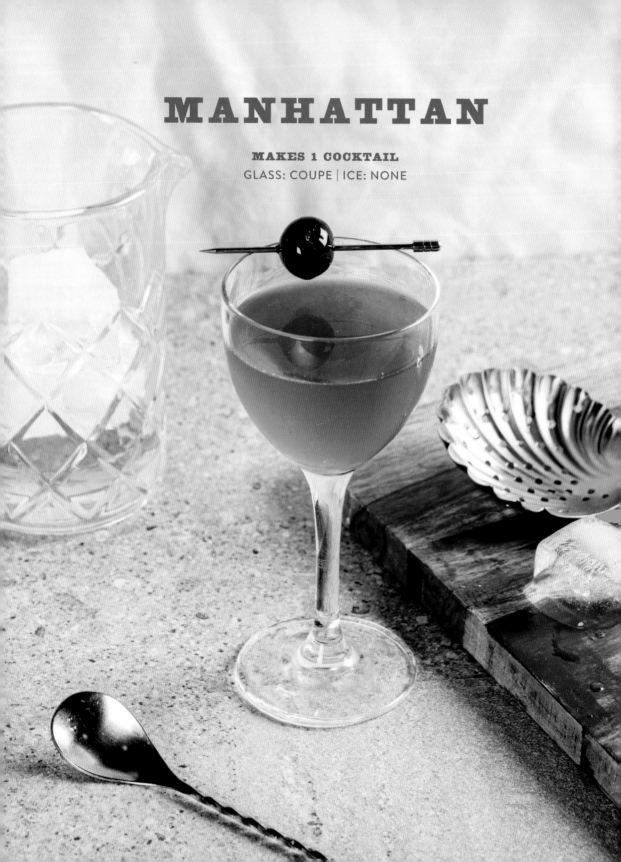

MANHATTAN

MAKES 1 COCKTAIL

GLASS: COUPE | ICE: NONE

2 ounces / 60 ml rye whiskey

1 ounce / 30 ml sweet vermouth

2 dashes Angostura Aromatic bitters

Garnish: Skewered Luxardo or Bourbon Cherry (page 90)

Chill the glass. Combine the ingredients with ice in a mixing glass and stir with a barspoon for 15 seconds. Strain the cocktail into the glass. Lay the skewered cherry across the rim and serve.

After the Martini, the Manhattan is likely the best recognized of the pre-Prohibition cocktails. Drink lore puts the first blending of whiskey, sweet vermouth, and bitters sometime around 1880, attributed to various New York hangouts for bon vivants and high-society types. It went by various names, too, including the Turf Club and the Jockey Club, but bartenders eventually settled on the Manhattan, which, according to David Wondrich, went on to survive "good times and bad, wars, recessions, Prohibition, the Depression, cultural upheavals, and, comfortingly, any number of truly terrible presidential administrations."

Today, the Manhattan is one of the most called-for cocktails in America, as smooth, supple, and timeless as a cashmere trench coat. Anyone who drinks or makes drinks for others should know how to put one together. A quick shortcut for remembering the recipe: 2-1-2. These are the Manhattan's measurements—2 ounces Bourbon, 1 ounce vermouth, 2 dashes bitters—as well as New York City's main area code. It should always be stirred, which creates a silky texture and prevents over-dilution, a side effect of shaking. In some cocktails, dilution is desirable. The Manhattan ain't one of those cocktails.

Changing up the types of whiskey, vermouth, and bitters will create different Manhattan profiles, but the best expression leans into the drink's robust nature: American or Canadian rye; Carpano Antica Formula, voluptuous with vanilla and spices; and Angostura, the workhorse of the bitters family. With the bitters, be judicious. Adding too much to a cocktail is like adding too much hot sauce to your eggs; they'll be all you taste.

ROB ROY

MAKES 1 COCKTAIL
GLASS: COUPE | ICE: NONE

Substitution of the base spirit is the most straightforward way to riff on a classic cocktail. That's what's happening here in the Rob Roy, a classic in its own right. Named for a Scottish folk hero, the drink invites Scotch to switch-hit for rye. Scotch whisky has a less intense flavor because it's aged in lightly toasted barrels, as opposed to the American and Canadian whiskies that rest in thoroughly charred ones. Match that softness with a lighter French vermouth.

2 ounces / 60 ml blended Scotch
1 ounce / 30 ml sweet vermouth
2 dashes Angostura Aromatic bitters
Garnish: Expressed lemon peel

Chill the glass. Combine the ingredients with ice in a mixing glass and stir with a barspoon for 15 seconds. Strain the cocktail into the glass. Express the lemon peel over the surface of the drink, rub it around the rim, drop it in the cocktail, and serve.

TIPPERARY

MAKES 1 COCKTAIL
GLASS: COUPE | ICE: NONE

Named for a county in Ireland, the Tipperary substitutes the base spirit of the Manhattan (Irish whiskey for rye) and introduces an extra modifier in the form of green Chartreuse. Chartreuse falls under the category of génépy, a family of herb-based French-Swiss Alpine liqueurs, and comes in green (the original) and yellow varieties. It's crafted from over 130 ingredients, and the Carthusian monks who've been making it for centuries aren't telling what those might be. Irish whiskey lacks the stage presence of its cousins, so you really taste the Chartreuse. It's a polarizing liqueur, so make sure you like it before investing in an expensive bottle.

1½ ounce / 45 ml Irish whiskey

1 ounce / 30 ml sweet vermouth

½ ounce / 15 ml green Chartreuse

2 dashes Angostura Aromatic bitters

Garnish: Expressed orange peel

Chill the glass. Combine the ingredients with ice in a mixing glass and stir with a barspoon for 15 seconds. Strain the cocktail into the glass. Express the orange peel over the surface of the drink, rub it around the rim, drop it in the cocktail, and serve.

THE NEW YORK FAMILY OF COCKTAILS

There's a classic cocktail named for each of the Big Apple's boroughs. The Brooklyn is a Manhattan with Maraschino and dry vermouth instead of sweet. The Bronx is a perfect Martini with a splash of orange juice; the Queens subs pineapple for orange. A drink for the fifth borough, Staten Island, came much later in the form of a stripped-down Piña Colada made from coconut rum and pineapple juice. It goes by the name Staten Island Ferry.

◀ Rob Roy, Tipperary, Breakfast Manhattan, Reversed

BREAKFAST MANHATTAN, REVERSED

MAKES 1 COCKTAIL
GLASS: COUPE | ICE: NONE

Nobody thinks "brunch" when they hear "Manhattan." Composed entirely of booze, the silky, sophisticated slow-sipper is best suited to long nights. To create a daytime-appropriate cocktail that preserves the Manhattan's Bourbon-vermouth DNA, this riff is built out as a reverse, which lowers the overall proof, with extra sweeteners in the forms of orange marmalade and maple syrup to further soften the whiskey's kick. The notes of citrus, maple, coffee, chocolate, and spice harmonize beautifully with the vermouth and Bourbon, creating a drink that just begs for a big plate of French toast.

A reverse refers to flip-flopping the proportions on a spirit-forward, two-ingredient cocktail. A Reverse Manhattan, for example, would call for 2 parts sweet vermouth and 1 part whiskey. This would be a great way to showcase a vermouth you really love or to lower the proof on a very strong drink. If you're having a second Manhattan, try making it a reverse so the last 10 minutes of the drink aren't so hard.

2 ounces / 60 ml Coffee Vermouth

1 ounce / 30 ml Bourbon

2 teaspoons orange marmalade

¼ ounce maple syrup

2 dashes Dashfire chocolate mole bitters

Garnish: Grated coffee bean, grated orange zest

Chill the glass. Combine the vermouth, Bourbon, and marmalade in a Boston shaker. Stir with a barspoon until the marmalade begins to dissolve. Add the maple syrup and ice and vigorously shake for 30 seconds. Strain the cocktail into the glass. Grate a coffee bean and orange over the surface of the drink and serve.

COFFEE VERMOUTH

MAKES 1 CUP / 236 ML

2 tablespoons freshly ground medium-roast coffee

1 cup / 236 ml sweet vermouth

Combine the ingredients in a French press coffee maker. Stir and allow to rest at room temperature for 2 hours. Press, strain, and bottle for future use.

WORKSHOP:
BOURBON CHERRIES

Popularized in the decades following Prohibition, fluorescent red "Maraschino" cherries add a retro crimson glow to the bottom of a cocktail, Manhattan or otherwise, but not a whole lot else. Quality Italian cocktail cherries, meanwhile, are delicious treasures waiting for you after the last sip. They're made from small, dense, sour cherries of the Marasca or Amarena species, packed in heavy burgundy syrup, and potted in antique-y ceramic crocks. We call for Luxardo cherries in this book, the same producer as Maraschino liqueur, but Fabbri and Toschi are other good brands. They're increasingly easy to find at cocktail emporiums and Italian specialty stores, but you can also make your own fancy cherries that will instantly give your Manhattan a professional polish.

MAKES ABOUT 1 QUART / 1 L

2½ pints sweet red cherries, washed, pitted, and stemmed

½ cup / 63 g confectioners' sugar

2 cups / 500 ml water

½ vanilla bean, slit lengthwise and scraped (substitute ¼ teaspoon vanilla extract)

2 cups / 400 g granulated sugar

5 ounces / 148 ml Bourbon

1 tablespoon strained lemon juice

Equipment: Large mixing bowl, medium pot, 1 quart/1 L glass jar

Combine the cherries and confectioners' sugar in a large mixing bowl and toss to evenly coat. Set the cherries aside to macerate. Bring the water to a rolling boil in a medium pot over medium-high heat. Add the vanilla bean and granulated sugar, gently stirring to dissolve. Reduce the heat to medium-low. Add the macerated cherries to the vanilla mixture and cook for 5 minutes. Reduce the heat to low. Stir in the Bourbon (and the vanilla extract, if using instead of bean) and simmer for 5 minutes, stirring occasionally. Remove the pot from heat and allow the cherries to cool for 10 minutes. Stir in the lemon juice and strain the mixture to separate the cherries from the syrup. Spoon the cherries into the jar and cover with the syrup. Seal the lid tightly and store the cherries in the fridge, where they will keep for 1 month.

Replace the Bourbon with brandy to make Brandied Cherries, a component in the Wisconsin Brandy Old Fashioned (page 71) and Armie Alexander (page 160).

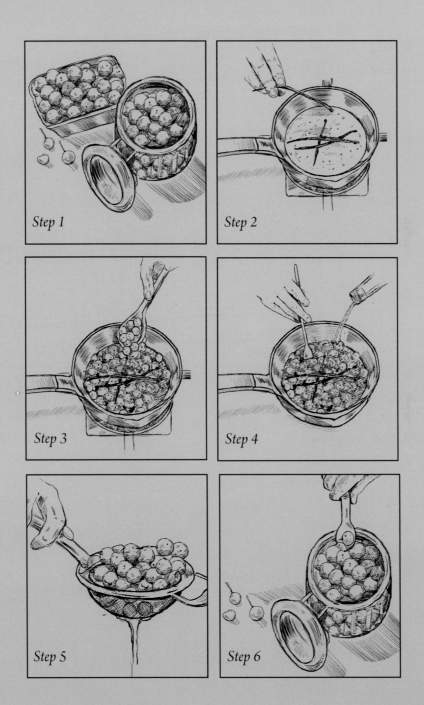

Step 1

Step 2

Step 3

Step 4

Step 5

Step 6

MARTINI

MAKES 1 COCKTAIL

GLASS: COUPE | ICE: NONE

3 ounces / 90 ml gin

½ ounce / 15 ml dry vermouth

Garnish: Expressed lemon peel or skewered green olive

Chill the glass. Combine the ingredients with ice in a mixing glass and stir with a barspoon for 15 seconds. Strain the cocktail into the glass. Express the lemon peel over the surface of the drink, rub it around the rim, drop it in the cocktail, and serve. Alternately, garnish with the olive and serve.

Nine out of 10 people, on hearing "classic cocktail," think first of the Martini. Codified by TV, movies, and marketing as the drink of dapper gents suavely swilling Martinis at their desks overlooking Madison Avenue, at long lunches in wood-clad supper clubs, and at dinner parties in their suburban sunken living rooms, the cocktail has become synonymous with a bygone era of sophistication and style.

As such, the Martini feels very tethered to the 1950s and '60s, but its origins are much older, dating back at least to the 1880s as a gin-and-sweet vermouth cocktail, perhaps one of the first riffs on the Manhattan. By the 1890s, bartenders began trading the established sweet (Italian) vermouth for newly trendy dry (French) vermouth, and the Martini evolved into the clear, dry thing we know today, one that "wraps the dude in a sweet, snoreless slumber," as poetically explained by the *Chicago Tribune* in 1893.

When you order a Martini, most bartenders will ask your preference for gin or vodka, though Martinis up until about the 1940s were made traditionally with the former. Vodka became popular in America during the US-Russia alliance of WWII, and the Martini was a natural fit, subbing one clear, high-proof spirit for another. But gin has flavor, while vodka is a neutral spirit, and a vodka Martini tastes like . . . alcohol. (Maybe that's why they're so often ordered dirtied with olive juice?) America's preference for gin over vodka inverted over the next 50 years, hitting a crescendo with the Martini bar boom of the 1990s; neutral vodka didn't get in the way of the sour apple, Key lime pie, and blue raspberry flavors lighting up our over-sized triangular glasses.

Fashions always swing back around eventually, and a Martini is once again best appreciated with gin. And since the recipe calls *only* for gin and dry vermouth, make sure you're using ones whose flavors you really enjoy. Having trouble deciding between all the options on the market? Try our favorite combo: a strong citric gin like Tanqueray Rangpur and a light French vermouth like Dolin.

PERFECT VESPER

MAKES 1 COCKTAIL
GLASS: COUPE | ICE: NONE

The Martini has long been associated with James Bond, but 007 actually created his own riff on the drink. In Sir Ian Fleming's 1953 caper Casino Royale, *Bond orders as follows: "Three measures of Gordon's [gin], one of vodka, half a measure of Kina Lillet. Shake it very well until it's ice-cold, then add a large thin slice of lemon peel." This variation on the Martini came to be known as the Vesper, which Bond later names for Vesper Lynd, his love interest in the novel. And like the beguiling double agent, it's a doozy. For a more modern approach, we build out the Vesper in a perfect, or equal parts, construction. Giving Lillet an even share of the glass helps defang the vodka and provides a fuller botanical bouquet that dovetails nicely with the gin. Make no mistake, though; like its namesake the all-booze Vesper can still be deadly.*

1 ounce / 30 ml gin
1 ounce / 30 ml vodka
1 ounce / 30 ml Lillet Blanc
Garnish: Pared lemon peel

Chill the glass. Combine the ingredients with ice in a mixing glass and stir with a barspoon for 15 seconds. Strain the cocktail into the glass. Place the lemon peel on the rim and serve.

BIJOU

Harry Johnson, author of 1882's New and Improved Bartender's Manual, *is the supposed inventor of this cocktail, which actually predates the Martini. The name is French for* jewel, *a reference to the precious stones representing each of the three ingredients: diamond for gin, sweet vermouth for ruby, green Chartreuse for emerald. The Bijou is botanical and fairly sweet up front, with the Chartreuse providing a pleasantly medicinal epilogue. Try replacing the sweet vermouth with dry for a less sweet, strikingly green cocktail.*

1 ounce / 30 ml gin

1 ounce / 30 ml sweet vermouth

1 ounce / 30 ml green Chartreuse

Garnish: Skewered Luxardo or
Bourbon Cherry (page 90)

Chill the glass. Combine the ingredients with ice in a mixing glass and stir with a barspoon for 15 seconds. Strain the cocktail into the glass. Lay the skewered cherry across the rim of the glass and serve.

◄ Perfect Vesper, Bijou, Martinez

MARTINEZ

As the Martini evolved through the decades, prevailing tastes stripped away its bells and whistles to eventually reveal something brisk and clear. The Martinez, popularized around 1884 courtesy O.H. Bryan's The Modern Bartender, *is probably what the proto-Martini looked like—which is to say, a lot like a Manhattan. But despite the ruddy-red appearance, the bracing gin backbone revealed on first sip is the cocktail's you-are-the-father moment. This drink calls for Old Tom, a style of gin with a distinct juniper profile and subtle caramel character from barrel aging, though feel free to try this with any gin. Maraschino liqueur, whose name comes from the Italian Marasca variety of cherry used in its production—no relation to the neon red ones filling bar caddies across America—adds an intriguing back-note of bubblegum.*

1½ ounces / 45 ml Old Tom gin

1½ ounces / 45 ml sweet vermouth

¼ ounces / 7 ml Luxardo Maraschino liqueur

2 dashes Angostura Aromatic bitters

Garnish: Expressed orange peel

Chill the glass. Combine the ingredients with ice in a mixing glass and stir with a barspoon for 15 seconds. Strain the cocktail into the glass. Express the orange peel over the surface of the drink, rub it around the rim, drop it in the cocktail, and serve.

GIN 101

GENEVER (Netherlands, 1500s) is gin's rich Dutch ancestor made from grain and flavored with juniper. Brand we like: Bols.

OLD TOM (England, early 1800s) is slightly sweetened and sometimes barrel-aged to create caramel complexity and viscous texture. Brand we like: Hayman's.

LONDON DRY (England, 1830s) is most people's idea of gin, its sugar stripped away and the juniper turned up. Brand we like: Beefeater.

WESTERN STYLE (UK and America, 1990s) is the new-school style made with fuller botanical profiles that de-emphasize juniper. Brands we like: Hendrick's (cucumber-forward), Blue Coat (citrus-forward), Tamworth Floral (flower-forward).

VARIATIONS ON THE GIN MARTINI

A martini ordered **SWEET** is made with more dry vermouth than usual.

A martini ordered **DRY** is made with less dry vermouth than usual.

A martini ordered **PERFECT** is made with equal parts of sweet and dry vermouths.

A martini ordered **FIFTY-FIFTY** is made with equal parts gin and dry vermouth. Orange bitters make it extra nice.

WORKSHOP:
VERMOUTH

What even is vermouth? Basically, it's plant wine. You start with a white-wine base; *fortify* it with a high-proof spirit (brandy, vodka); and *aromatize* it for a period of time with some combination of plant life: herbs, barks, roots, flowers, spices, etc. One nonnegotiable component is wormwood, the herbaceous, bitter plant most associated with absinthe. Early vermouth formulas, which were used as medical tonics, contained wormwood—or *wermut* in German, the bungled pronunciation of which eventually gave vermouth its modern name. Wormwood isn't often used in contemporary commercial formulas, but we think of its presence in our recipe as a historical callback. You can find it in spice shops and online. (No, it will not make you hallucinate.)

Step 1

Step 2

Step 3

MAKES ABOUT 3³/₄ CUPS / 868 ML

1 (750 ml) bottle Pinot Grigio

4 ounces / 120 ml vodka

1 teaspoon dried wormwood

¼ teaspoon dried gentian root

¼ teaspoon dried angelica root

¼ teaspoon dried cinchona bark

¼ teaspoon dried sage

¼ teaspoon dried rosemary

¼ teaspoon dried thyme

¼ teaspoon dried chamomile

½ tablespoon dried bitter orange peel

1 tablespoon orange zest

1 tablespoon lemon zest

1 teaspoon grated ginger

4 cloves, toasted and lightly crushed

1 star anise, toasted and lightly crushed

Equipment: 2 quart/1.9 L glass jar, fine-mesh strainer, 1 quart/ 1 L glass bottle

Combine all the ingredients in the jar. Shake gently to make sure the dried ingredients soak evenly. Store the mixture in a cool, dark place for 2 weeks, gently shaking once a day. After the allotted time, strain the mixture through a fine-mesh strainer, reserving the liquid and discarding the solids. Bottle the finished vermouth in a clean glass bottle and store in the fridge between uses.

SPRITZ

MAKES 1 COCKTAIL
GLASS: RED WINE | ICE: LARGE CUBE X 4

3 ounces / 90 ml prosecco or other dry sparkling white wine

2 ounces / 60 ml aperitif of choice

1 ounce / 30 ml seltzer

Garnish: Orange slice

Set up the glass with the ice. Add the ingredients and briskly stir with a barspoon for 5 seconds. Garnish with the orange and serve.

Y ou need five components to make a Spritz: ice + seltzer + wine (typically sparkling) + amaro or aperitivo, the intermarried categories of bitter, usually European liqueurs made primarily from herbs, flowers, spices, and barks + garnish. To be ready to whip up a Spritz at any moment, commit this handy acronym to memory: I SWAG. And yes, player, you do.

Not every Spritz is an Aperol Spritz. In fact, neither the classic recipe you'll find here, nor the riffs that follow, call specifically for the famous carmine aperitivo, more or less a lower-proof analogue to Campari. Throughout Italian bars and cafés, where Spritz culture unfurls during the leisurely golden hours after work and before dinner, Aperol didn't become synonymous with the Spritz until the 1990s. According to Talia Baiocchi and Leslie Pariseau, authors of the excellent cocktail book *Spritz:*

> While the spritz had been the most popular aperitivo drink in the Veneto and many parts of Friuli and Alto Adige for decades, it's not until Aperol began marketing the spritz in the 1990s that it went from being a mostly local ritual to Italy's most popular cocktail. [. . .] When Aperol first began marketing the drink in the 1990s, the spritz made up "10 percent of the sales volume of Aperol," says [former Aperol marketing director, Vito] Casoni. Today it is the primary way in which Aperol is consumed, worldwide.

Aperol's marketing smarts coupled with the surging popularity of prosecco, the Italian sparkling wine, made the Aperol Spritz a phenomenon throughout Italy that was eventually exported abroad. But it's important to note that—no disrespect to

Aperol—there is a whole spectrum of spritzing beyond that one distinctive bottle. "Just as there are a million tiny rituals in Italy, there are also a million tiny allegiances," Baiocchi and Pariseau write. "If you are in Venice your spritz will often be served with Select; in Padua it's Aperol; in Brescia it might be Cappelletti Aperitivo, and so on."

With hundreds of different possible combinations, the best way to find the flavor profile you most prefer is to experiment with different amari and aperitivi. The matrix below organizes 10 terrific options by proof and flavor. Pick one that sounds good to you and drop it into the classic 3-2-1 formula in the recipe, then get into the riffs that follow, which switch up the bubbles and introduce various modifiers.

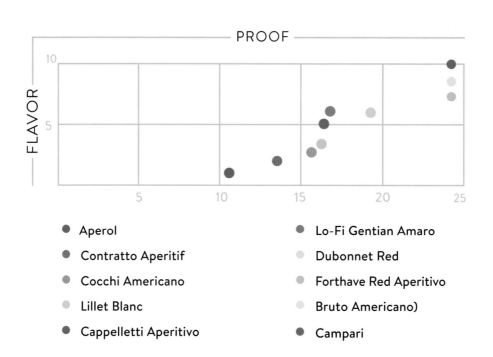

Modena Spritz, Alps Spritz, Rosé Royale Spritz ▶

MODENA SPRITZ

MAKES 1 COCKTAIL
GLASS: RED WINE | ICE: LARGE CUBE X 4

The Spritz is endlessly riff-able by mixing up the aperitif and the wine. A sharp original pairing is Lambrusco, the family of burgundy firecrackers from Emilia-Romagna, and Vecchio del Capo, a subtle Calabrese amaro with notes of chamomile and licorice. Lambrusco comes in a wide spectrum of sugar expressions, from trendily bone-dry to so sweet you might as well be drinking grape soda. Shoot for something in the middle, like Famiglia Carafoli's "Nicchia." It's got mega sparkle, voluptuous berry-plum flavor, and a balance of sweetness, tannins, and acidity.

3 ounces / 90 ml off-dry Lambrusco

2 ounces / 60 ml Vecchio del Capo amaro

1 ounce / 30 ml seltzer

Garnish: Strawberry

Set up the glass with the ice. Add the ingredients and briskly stir with a barspoon for 5 seconds. Garnish with the strawberry and serve.

ALPS SPRITZ

On the herb-and-wildflower-carpeted foothills of the French Alps, people have been brewing wines and liqueurs from the native flora for centuries. One of the more obscure—but newly en vogue in the cocktail world—is génépy, whose 30-odd botanicals include a silvery sage-like strain of artemisia. The liqueur stands in for amaro in this white Spritz, its herbal and floral notes laced together with a misting of chamomile tea. There are several génépy producers on the market, but for this recipe we recommend Dolin Génépy le Chamois, whose formula dates to 1821.

3 ounces / 90 ml Crémant

2 ounces / 60 ml génépy

1 ounce / 30 ml seltzer

Chamomile Mist

Garnish: Expressed thyme sprig, expressed orange peel

Set up the glass with the ice. Add the ingredients and briskly stir with a bar-spoon for 5 seconds. Spray the Chamomile Mist across the surface of the drink and outside of the glass. Garnish with the thyme. Express the orange peel over the surface of the drink, rub it around the rim, drop it in the cocktail, and serve.

CHAMOMILE MIST

1 chamomile tea bag

¾ cup / 177 ml boiling water

Brew the tea in the boiling water for 5 minutes. When it has cooled completely, transfer it to an atomizer or spray bottle and reserve at room temperature.

ROSÉ ROYALE SPRITZ

MAKES 1 COCKTAIL
GLASS: RED WINE | ICE: LARGE CUBE X 4

Inexpensive Italian prosecco or Spanish cava will get the job done in any Spritz, but when you want a version that's dressed up for a night on the town (or pool party at a villa), pop a bottle of rosé Champagne. The rose-gold bubbles not only look regal as hell, but also introduce berry and toasted-brioche notes you're never going to get from steel-tanked sparkling wines.

3 ounces / 90 ml brut rosé Champagne

1 ounce / 30 ml Nonino amaro

1 ounce / 30 ml Watermelon Juice
(page 37)

½ ounce / 15 ml Rhubarb Shrub

1 ounce / 30 ml seltzer

Garnish: Watermelon slice

Set up the glass with the ice. Add the ingredients and briskly stir with a barspoon for 5 seconds. Garnish with the watermelon slice and serve.

RHUBARB SHRUB
MAKES ABOUT 2½ CUPS / 590 ML

2 rhubarb stalks, peeled and cut
in 1 inch / 2.5 cm pieces

1 cup / 200 g granulated sugar

1 cup / 236 ml Champagne Vinegar

1 cup / 236 ml water

Toss the rhubarb with the sugar in a medium mixing bowl and cover it with plastic wrap. Let the fruit macerate at room temperature for 3 days, stirring once a day, while the juices of the rhubarb combine with the sugar to make a syrup. Strain off and reserve the syrup, pressing as much liquid out as possible. Combine the reserved syrup, vinegar, and water in an airtight container and store in the refrigerator, where the shrub will keep for 6 months.

CHAMPAGNE VINEGAR
MAKES ABOUT 1 CUP / 236 ML

1½ cups / 354 ml Champagne

1 ounce / 30 ml raw apple cider vinegar
(with the mother), such as Bragg

Combine the ingredients in a glass jar, cover it with cheesecloth or a coffee filter, and screw on the lid. Move the jar to a dark place and allow it to ferment into vinegar. This could take up 3 months, depending on variable conditions, but begin tasting at 3 weeks.

WORKSHOP:
VERJUS

A contraction of the French *vert* (green) and *jus* (juice), verjus is the liquid wrung from unripe grapes. It's also the solution to a problem: What's a winemaker to do when they have too much fruit on the vine? Maybe there are more grapes than they can process into wine; maybe the overabundance is spreading the nutrients too thin. It's likely both are true, which is why growers thin out grapes while they're still unripe. Pressing verjus from the green grapes—even ones that ripen red are green at this stage—turns waste into gold. The nectar has a fruity, mellow acidity that can be used like vinegar or citrus juice in cooking and cocktails.

Unripe grapes aren't exactly something you find in the supermarket. Your best bet is to reach out to a grower at your local farmers' market or contact a nearby winery. When making verjus, it's important to work quickly as the juice will begin to oxidize and turn brown. The sooner you get it strained, bottled, and chilled, the better it will hold its greenish-gold color.

Our verjus recipe below introduces a second layer of flavor and aroma with orange and lemon peels, which is not traditional but is especially effective for mixing drinks. Feel free to leave them out if you want something purer, or experiment with other aromatics, like lemongrass, blood orange, or bergamot tea.

ACTIVE TIME: 30 MINUTES | TOTAL PROJECT TIME: 24 HOURS

MAKES ABOUT 1 QUART / 1 L

3 oranges

2 lemons

5 pounds / 2.3 kg unripe white wine grapes

½ teaspoon citric acid

Equipment: Vegetable peeler, food processor or food mill, strainer, 1 quart/1 L airtight container x 2

Remove the peels of the lemons and oranges with a vegetable peeler, careful to leave all the bitter white pith behind, and reserve. Pulse the grapes in a food processor or run them through a food mill to release as much juice as possible. Working quickly to prevent oxidation, strain the crushed grapes through a fine-mesh strainer at least twice to separate as much of the pulp and skins from the juice as possible. Transfer the juice to an airtight container and express and add the citrus peels to the juice. Chill the mixture in the refrigerator for 24 hours, then strain off and discard the peels. Transfer the finished verjus to an airtight container, stir in the citric acid, and store in the refrigerator, where it will keep for several months.

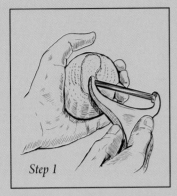

Step 1

Step 2

Step 3

Step 4

Step 5

VERJUS SPRITZ

MAKES 1 COCKTAIL

GLASS: RED WINE | ICE: LARGE CUBE X 4

3 ounces / 90 ml cava

1 ounce / 30 ml Cointreau

¾ ounce / 22 ml Aperol

¾ ounce / 22 ml Citrus Verjus

Garnish: Grapefruit slice, spearmint sprig

Set up the glass with the ice. Add the ingredients and briskly stir with a barspoon for 5 seconds. Garnish with the grapefruit and mint and serve.

DAIQUIRI

2 ounces / 60 ml white rum

¾ ounces / 22 ml strained lime juice

¾ ounces / 22 ml Simple Syrup (page 4)

Garnish: Expressed lime peel

Chill the glass. Combine the ingredients in a Boston shaker with ice and vigorously shake for 20 seconds. Strain the cocktail into the glass, express lime peel over the surface, and serve.

For some, the word conjures circa-1980s happy hours at TGI Fridays or conga lines on a Carnival cruise. For others, it brings to mind Ernest Hemingway, linen suits, and the suave sultriness of mid-century Havana. *Daiquiri* is as loaded as a bootlegger's pistol, twinned to associations of gauche excess and torpid sophistication. All depends on your perspective. But the Daiquiri's backstory goes beyond either picture, reaching deep into the southeastern corner of Cuba in the sundown of the 19th century.

The Spanish-American War in Cuba had just ended in a US victory that included Spain's ceding its territories of Puerto Rico, the Philippines, and Cuba. Eager to exploit Cuba's unmined caches of iron ore, American engineering expeditions turned the Sierra Maestra near a village called Daiquirí into Swiss cheese. There was money to be made in Cuba.

Jennings Stockton Cox was one of the lead engineers on the Sierra Maestra mine. Though how he arrived at combining rum, citrus juice, and sugar—an adaptation of the popular local Canchanchara cocktail, a stirred honey-sweetened highball—is debated, Cox is the drink's undisputed author. According to his journal, Cox's Daiquiri was batched to serve six and fizzed with a dose of mineral water. His handwritten recipe also mentions lemon, not lime, perhaps a phonetic spelling of the Spanish *limón*.

The Daiquiri traveled back to the States in 1909 with a Spanish-American War veteran named Lucius Johnson, who preached the cocktail's virtues to his pals at D.C.'s Army & Navy Club. (The Club's bar, the Daiquiri Room, took the drink as its namesake, and a plaque commemorates Johnson's introduction.) Meanwhile, the Daiquiri was spreading around Cuba, where *cantineros* reverse-engineered Cox's serves-six formula into single-drink proportions and nixed the bubbles along the way, streamlining it into the sharp, luminous cooler that's considered such a classic today.

GUARAPO DAIQUIRI

This Daiquiri is all about bringing rum back to its essential ingredient: sugarcane, the juice from which is called guarapo *in Spanish. In this riff, sugarcane juice takes the place of Simple Syrup, and grassy, barnyardy rhum agricole takes the place of neutral white rum, creating a more dynamic drink. Seek out freshly pressed guarapo at farmers' markets and juice bars, or buy whole cane—groceries specializing in Latin, African, Caribbean, or South and Southeast Asian ingredients should have it—and juice it at home. Sugarcane Island Company also ships six-packs of its pure cane juice across the country.*

2 ounces / 60 ml rhum agricole

¾ ounces / 22 ml strained lime juice

¾ ounces / 22 ml strained sugarcane juice

3 dashes Fee Bros. molasses bitters

Garnish: Pared lime peel

Chill the glass. Combine the ingredients in a Boston shaker with ice and vigorously shake for 20 seconds. Strain the cocktail into the glass, place the lime peel on the rim, and serve.

THE HEMINGWAY SPECIAL

Ernest Hemingway's predilection for rum was famous in Havana, especially at his favorite haunt, El Floridita, where the *cantineros* would tweak and twist the basic rum-sugar-lime recipe. One of those twists, the Hemingway Special, has become a classic cocktail in its own right, though in modern times it goes by the name Hemingway Daiquiri. To make this version, combine the same measure of rum and lime juice, add a ½ ounce/15 ml each of strained grapefruit juice and Maraschino liqueur, omit the Simple Syrup, and mix according to the directions above. This makes for a stronger (fitting for Hemingway) and more complex version of the original Daiquiri, with nuttiness from the Maraschino and juicy bitterness from the grapefruit adding layers of flavor as well as balancing out the extremes of rum and lime in the absence of the sugar.

Guarapo Daiquiri, Bonfire of the Daiquiris, Sesamint Daiquiri ▶

BONFIRE OF THE DAIQUIRIS

MAKES 1 COCKTAIL

GLASS: COUPE | ICE: NONE

The relationship between the thirsty sailors of the British navy and Caribbean rum goes way back. The term Navy Strength refers to a rum with 57 percent proof. For a quality bottle we recommend Smith & Cross. In business since 1788, their Navy Strength tastes like a flambéed slice of extravagantly spiced banana bread and is showcased well in this richer, darker Daiquiri.

2 ounces / 60 ml Jamaican Navy Strength rum

¾ ounce / 22 ml strained lime juice

¾ ounce / 22 ml Demerara Syrup (page 4)

Garnish: Float (page 196) overproof Jamaican rum, Cinnamon Ignition (page 196)

Chill the glass. Combine the ingredients in a Boston shaker with ice and vigorously shake for 15 seconds. Strain the cocktail into the glass. Garnish with rum float and Cinnamon Ignition and serve.

SESAMINT DAIQUIRI

Pop quiz: When someone says they don't like frozen Daiquiris they are (a) a liar, (b) a snob, (c) legitimately frightened by the quality of most frozen daiquiris, or (d) any of the above. If you guessed (d), congrats. While it's a sad fact that the majority of frozen daiquiris are artificial, oversweetened offenders, one that's properly made can be just as satisfying—even more so on a very hot day—as the classic that cocktail sophisticates have so overwhelmingly embraced. This version builds on sekanjabin, a shrub-like Iranian beverage made with honey, vinegar, and mint, and is crazy refreshing with just a hint of salinity and sesame savoriness.

4 ounces / 120 ml white rum

1½ ounces / 45 ml strained lime juice

1½ ounces / 45 ml Sekanjabin

¼ ounce / 7 ml Toasted Sesame Saline

20 ounces / 570 g ice, about 5 cups

Garnish: Expressed spearmint bunch x 2, metal straw x 2

Combine all the ingredients in a blender and blend until smooth and frosty. Divide the cocktail between the glasses, garnish each with the mint and a straw, and serve.

SEKANJABIN

MAKES ABOUT 2 CUPS / 470 ML

1 cup / 236 ml water

1⅓ cups / 454 g honey

⅔ cup / 157 ml distilled white vinegar

30 large spearmint leaves

Bring the water to a boil over high heat in a small saucepan. Add the honey and reduce the heat to low, continuously stirring to dissolve the honey. Remove from heat and stir in the vinegar. Add the mint to a heat-safe jar. Slowly pour the honey mixture into the jar and tightly seal. Gently shake for 10 seconds. Reserve the syrup at room temperature, allowing the mint to infuse for 1 hour. Strain off and discard the mint. Return the finished sekanjabin to the jar, allow it to completely cool, and transfer it to the refrigerator, where it will keep for 2 weeks.

TOASTED SESAME SALINE

MAKES 4 OUNCES / 120 ML

1 tablespoon sesame seeds

4 ounces / 120 ml water

1 tablespoon Morton's kosher salt

Add the sesame seeds to a shallow pan and place over medium heat. Allow the seeds to toast, stirring to prevent burning, until they turn a rich orange-tan color, 1 to 2 minutes. Remove the seeds immediately from the heat, transferring to a cool tray or plate to stop the cooking. Bring the water to a boil in a small pot over medium-high heat. Add the salt, stirring to dissolve. Remove the salt water from the heat and transfer to a heat-safe lidded jar, like a canning jar. Add the toasted sesame seeds to the jar, seal it tightly, and gently shake for 10 seconds. Allow the mixture to cool to room temperature, then move it to the refrigerator to infuse for 24 hours. Strain off and discard the sesame seeds, reserving the finished saline in the jar. This will keep refrigerated for 2 weeks.

WORKSHOP:
ACID ADJUSTING

T art, tangy, acidic—whatever you call it, the experience of sourness is an essential and balancing component in many classic cocktails. As juices go, lemon and lime rule as souring agents. But what if you don't want your cocktail to taste like lemon or lime? What if you want it to taste like, say, orange or pineapple or grapefruit? These vitamin C heavy hitters are innately acidic but have too much natural sugar to effectively convey sourness in a drink.

The godfather of the acid-adjusting technique is Dave Arnold, who ran New York City's forward-thinking Booker and Dax cocktail bar from 2012 to 2016. By adding citric or malic acid to a fruit juice or puree, you can manipulate its acidity to match that of a lemon or lime, while still preserving the other flavors in that fruit. Imagine, for example, a Margarita with the tropical caress of pineapple but the same tart punch as if it had been made with lime juice—or, in the recipe below, a Strawberry Daiquiri. Acid adjusting turns a drink that's basically a vehicle for sugar into one with barely any sweetness at all. It's a mind trip.

ACID-ADJUSTED STRAWBERRIES

TOTAL PROJECT TIME: 5 MINUTES

MAKES ABOUT 1 CUP / 236 ML

1 pint strawberries, stemmed and hulled

2 tablespoons powdered citric acid

Equipment: high-powered blender, fine-mesh strainer, 1 pint/470 ml airtight container

Puree berries in a blender until very smooth. Run the puree through a fine-mesh strainer to remove the seeds. Measure out 1 cup/236 ml of the puree and add the citric acid, stirring to completely dissolve. Transfer to an airtight container and store in the refrigerator, where it will keep 2 weeks.

Step 1

Step 2

Step 3

ACID-ADJUSTED STRAWBERRY DAIQUIRI

MAKES 1 COCKTAIL

GLASS: ROCKS | ICE: CRUSHED
OR PEBBLE

2 ounces / 60 ml white rum

2 ounces / 60 ml Acid-Adjusted
Strawberry Puree

¼ ounce / 7 ml strained lime juice

Garnish: Strawberry

Combine the ingredients in a Boston
shaker with ice and vigorously shake
for 20 seconds. Pack the glass with the
ice. Strain the cocktail over the ice and
mound more ice on top. Garnish with a
strawberry and serve.

PISCO SOUR

MAKES 1 COCKTAIL

GLASS: COUPE | ICE: NONE

1½ ounces / 45 ml Peruvian pisco

1 ounce / 30 ml strained lemon juice

¾ ounce / 22 ml Simple Syrup (page 4)

Whites from 1 large egg

Garnish: 3 drops Amargo Chuncho bitters

Chill the glass. Combine the ingredients in a Boston shaker and vigorously dry-shake for 30 seconds. Add ice to the shaker and shake for 15 seconds and strain the cocktail into the glass. Drop the bitters in a triangle pattern in the middle of the drink's foamy surface. Drag a toothpick in circle through their centers to create leaf pattern. Serve.

For centuries, next-door neighbors Peru and Chile have been squabbling about who produced pisco first. Each country has different grape preferences and regulations—Peruvian pisco, for example, cannot be aged in wood and is always gin-clear, whereas in Chile barrel resting is permitted—but regardless of the differences, they share a common vehicle for showcasing their national drinks: the Pisco Sour.

History long held Victor Morris, a circa-1903 Salt Lake City émigré to Peru who worked on the railroads, as the inventor of the Pisco Sour. Morris, the story goes, was mixing Whiskey Sours at a railway line inauguration, ran out of whiskey, and swapped in Peru's native spirit, pisco. It proved a serendipitous substitution, as he parlayed the fame into his own bar, Morris' Bar, which he operated in Lima until 1929. There's a whiff of colonialism to this story, but maybe more so to the fact that it was long held up as the definitive account of the Pisco Sour's genesis. The excerpt on page 121 from a Peruvian cookbook published in 1903 indicates the Pisco Sour predated Morris's arrival in South America. The cookbook calls the drink, simply, "Cocktail."

Like other Sour cocktails, the Pisco works off the formula of spirit, citrus, sugar, and egg white, though it's typically served straight up instead of on the rocks like the Whiskey Sour (page 76). The brisk bite and grapey aromas of the pisco soar through the tart drink. The classic recipe and some of the riffs that follow specifically call for Amargo Chuncho bitters, which are made with Amazonian flora, but Angostura will work in a pinch. Three careful drops on the cocktail's foamed surface, either in a symmetrical line or forming the points on a triangle, are traditional.

DASHES VS. DROPS

Throughout this book, we call for bitters in both dashes and drops. The difference? Dashes are added while mixing. Drops are added as a garnish.

PISCO SOURSOP FIZZ

MAKES 1 COCKTAIL

GLASS: COLLINS | ICE: STANDARD CUBES

Soursop, also known as guanabana, has the most intriguing flavor, like a tangy, custardy cross between passion fruit, guava, and very ripe bananas. A little soursop goes a long way, its juice performing three tasks in one in this equatorial overlay on the Pisco Sour: sweetening (most commercially available guanabana juice contains added sugar), reprogramming the acidity, and modifying the overall flavor with its captivating je ne sais quoi.

2 ounces / 60 ml soursop juice

1½ ounces / 45 ml Peruvian pisco

½ ounce / 15 ml strained lemon juice

4 dashes Amargo Chuncho bitters

Seltzer to top, 1 to 2 ounces/30-60 ml

Garnish: Lemon wheel

Set up the glass with the ice. Combine all the ingredients except for the seltzer in the glass and briskly stir with a barspoon for 10 seconds. Top with the seltzer, garnish with the lemon, and serve.

CHILCANO SOUR

MAKES 1 COCKTAIL
GLASS: COUPE | ICE: NONE

The Chilcano is a fizzy, refreshing Peruvian highball made with pisco, bitters, lime juice, and ginger ale. Here are the same and similar ingredients remixed into a Sour format, the main alteration being turning the ginger soda into a ginger syrup that gives the Chilcano Sour a distinctive zip. While we would normally advocate for using fresh ginger in a cocktail syrup, simply simmering bottled ginger beer with sugar is an easy and very effective shortcut. You want the spiciest ginger beer you can find; look for Reed's "strongest" variety or the British brand Fever-Tree. In a pinch, Liber & Co.'s Fiery Ginger Syrup can be substituted for homemade.

1½ ounces / 45 ml Peruvian pisco

1 ounce / 30 ml strained lemon juice

¾ ounce / 22 ml Quick Ginger Syrup

Whites from 1 large egg

Garnish: 3 drops Amargo Chuncho bitters

Chill the glass. Combine the ingredients in a Boston shaker and vigorously dry-shake for 30 seconds. Add ice to the shaker and shake for 15 seconds. Strain the cocktail into the glass. Drop the bitters in a triangle pattern in the middle of the drink's foamy surface and serve.

QUICK GINGER SYRUP

MAKES ABOUT 2 CUPS / 470 ML

1½ cups / 350 ml bottled extra-spicy ginger beer

1½ cups / 300 g granulated sugar

Bring the ginger beer to a simmer in a small saucepot over medium-low heat. Add the sugar, stirring to completely dissolve. Allow the finished ginger syrup to completely cool, then transfer to an airtight container and store in the refrigerator, where it will keep for 2 weeks.

◀ Pisco Soursop Fizz, Chilcano Sour, Ps & Ts Sour

Ps & Ts SOUR

MAKES 1 COCKTAIL

GLASS: COUPE | ICE: NONE

Unlike in Peru, where the virginal piscos never touch wood, Chile permits its pisco makers to age their brandies in barrels. The Ps & Ts Sour is a showcase for this aged Chilean pisco, whose confident maple-vanilla-caramel character can keep up with the kinds of bossy ingredients (peanut, tamarind, turmeric) that would overwhelm most Peruvian piscos.

1½ ounces / 45 ml aged pisco, such as Pisco Mistal Nobel Reservado Extra Añejado

1 ounce / 30 ml Tamarind-Turmeric Cordial

¾ ounce / 22 ml strained lemon juice

8 drops Peanut Tincture

White from 1 large egg

Garnish: 5 drops Amargo Chuncho bitters

Chill the glass. Combine the ingredients in a Boston shaker and vigorously dry-shake for 30 seconds. Add ice to the shaker and shake for 15 seconds. Strain the cocktail into the glass. Drop the bitters in the middle of the drink's foamy surface to create a large circle. Drag a toothpick outward from the center of the circle to create a star pattern and serve.

TAMARIND-TURMERIC CORDIAL

MAKES ABOUT 1¼ CUPS / 296 ML

1 cup / 236 ml vodka

½ cup / 100 g granulated sugar

2 tablespoons tamarind paste

2 tablespoons freshly grated turmeric

Warm the vodka over low heat in a small saucepot. Add the sugar and tamarind, stirring to completely dissolve. Add the turmeric and simmer over low heat for 10 minutes. Remove the pot from the heat, cover, and allow the mixture to cool for 20 minutes. Transfer it to an airtight container, gently shake for 5 seconds, and store at room temperature in a cool, dark place for 24 hours. Strain off and discard any solids and return the finished cordial to the airtight container. Store in the refrigerator, where it will keep for 1 month.

PEANUT TINCTURE

MAKES ABOUT 4 OUNCES / 120 ML

2 tablespoons unsalted peanuts, crushed

4 ounces / 120 ml white rum

Combine the ingredients in an airtight container, gently agitate, and allow them to infuse at room temperature for 24 hours. Strain the mixture through a fine-mesh strainer and transfer the finished tincture to a small eyedropper bottle. Store in a cool, dark place. This will keep indefinitely, but the peanut flavor will begin to degrade after 2 months.

An egg, a glass of pisco, a teaspoon of fine sugar and a squeeze of lime, will open up a good appetite.

—TRANSLATED FROM *NUEVO MANUAL DE COCINA A LA CRIOLLA*, 1903

WORKSHOP:
AROMATIC BITTERS

Bitterness and sweetness, inversions of one another, are fatefully twinned in the most essential of cocktails. Bitterness can come in the form of amari, like Campari in the Negroni (page 50), Fernet-Branca in the Menta Julep (page 34), or Averna in the El Capilla (page 185), but most often bitterness is introduced through bitters, the concoctions of aromatics steeped in alcohol that deliver depth charges of flavor and fragrance in just a few dashes or drops.

Over the last decade, dozens upon dozens of bitters boutiques have exploded the market to join heritage brands like Angostura, Peychaud's, and Fee Bros., all of which are called for in various recipes throughout the book. These days, if you can think of a flavor (bay leaf, passion fruit, chipotle), there's a bitters brewer out there making it. But you can also make your own with very little effort. All it takes is the willingness to source some unusual ingredients and patience.

Our base recipe for aromatic bitters is a broad-spectrum formula with a top-note of red fruits that will work as well in a Pisco Sour as it will in a Manhattan (page 84). What's cool about making your own bitters is that you can customize the profile to suit your preferences, so feel free to play around with the baseline below.

ACTIVE TIME: 10 MINUTES | TOTAL PROJECT TIME: 2 TO 4 WEEKS

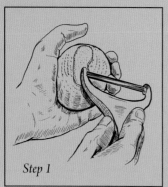

Step 1

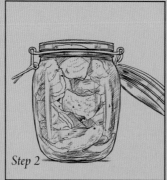

Step 2

Step 3

MAKES ABOUT 1¼ CUPS / 296 ML

1 orange

1 tablespoon dried bitter orange peel

6 cloves

2 nutmeg, cracked

1 cinnamon stick, cracked

2 star anise, cracked

1 tablespoon dried hibiscus

2½ tablespoons dried sweet cherries

2 tablespoons raisins

1 tablespoon cacao nibs

1 tablespoon dried gentian root

1½ tablespoons dried sarsaparilla bark

1 teaspoon dried cherry bark

1 teaspoon dried birch bark

1 tablespoon dried cinchona bark

Overproof rum to cover, about
1¼ cups / 296 ml

Equipment: Vegetable peeler,
2 cup/470 ml airtight container,
fine-mesh strainer, eyedropper
bottle

Remove the peel from the orange with a vegetable peeler, careful to leave all the bitter white pith behind, and add it to an airtight container with the remaining ingredients. Transfer the container to a cool, dark place and allow the aromatics to steep in the rum for 2 to 4 weeks, checking the intensity of the flavor once a week until the desired intensity is reached. Strain the mixture twice through a fine-mesh strainer, discarding the solids. Transfer the finished bitters to an eyedropper bottle and store at room temperature, where they will keep indefinitely.

TWEAK IT

CITRUS BITTERS: Add the peels of 1 grapefruit, 2 lemons, and 2 limes.

JAMAICAN BITTERS: Add 1 tablespoon each of whole allspice, thyme leaves, and grated ginger, plus 1 halved Scotch bonnet chile.

PROVENÇAL BITTERS: Add 4 sprigs rosemary, 6 sprigs tarragon, 1 tablespoon dried lavender, and 1 teaspoon fennel seed.

EL PRESIDENTE

1½ ounces / 45 ml white rum

¾ ounce / 22 ml dry Curaçao

¾ ounce / 22 ml blanc vermouth

Dash grenadine

Garnish: Expressed orange peel

Chill the glass. Combine the ingredients with ice in a mixing glass and stir with a barspoon for 30 seconds. Strain the cocktail into the glass. Express the orange peel over the surface of the drink, rub it around the rim, drop it in the cocktail, and serve.

The Daiquiri (page 108) might be more famous, but it's not the only classic to come out of Cuba, whose cocktail culture thrived during American Prohibition. While many bartenders jetted to Europe to ride out the dry spell, "much closer to home … 90 miles off the Florida coast, affluent Americans gallivanted off in droves to a place where both the literal and tippling climates were warmer," *Washington Post* spirits columnist M. Carrie Allan wrote in 2019. "Prohibition didn't stop Americans from drinking, but it did a heck of a lot for the tourism industry in pre-revolutionary Cuba."

Enter El Presidente, a sophisticated stirred rum cocktail allegedly named for Mario García Menocal, Cuba's president from 1913 to 1921. The drink first appears in the 1915 *Manual del Cantinero,* the bible curated by the island's esteemed bartending association. At its essence, this is a rum-and-vermouth drink blushed with grenadine. The addition of Curaçao came a few years later when, according to legend, Cuba's next president demanded his own version of the drink. The citrus notes it introduces make the cocktail more complex without overwhelming the rum. Either way you'll understand why American society reporter Basil Yoon described El Presidente in his 1928 book *When It's Cocktail Time in Cuba* as "the aristocrat of cocktails."

THE OTHER VERMOUTH

Following the 1915 formula, our Presidente calls for blanc (in France) or bianco (in Italy) vermouth. Blancs are clear like dry vermouths, but sweet—though not as sweet as sweet vermouths—with suggestions of melon, elderflower, and vanilla. Cuban *cantineros* of the era referred to this style as vermouth de Chambery, the Alpine city where Dolin has produced vermouth since 1821. According to David Wondrich, writing for *Imbibe!* magazine, blanc "is the style for which the southeastern French town of Chambery was historically known." El Presidente makes a fine introduction to blanc vermouth. Try it substituted for Lillet in a White Negroni (page 53) or Perfect Vesper (page 94) or spritzed with seltzer or tonic and garnished with a sliced strawberry. We like Dolin's floral blanc, while Italian biancos from Cocchi and Carpano tend to be more vanilla-forward.

HAIL TO THE CHIEF

MAKES 1 COCKTAIL

GLASS: SNIFTER | ICE: NONE

The simple tweak on the El Presidente rolls out the barrels, so to speak, with añejo rum—we recommend Ron del Barrilito 3 Star from Puerto Rico, which is rested in vintage sherry barrels—and Grand Marnier, the Cognac-kissed orange liqueur. Paired with perfect proportions of dry and sweet vermouths and the requisite dash of grenadine, they direct the Hail to the Chief into richer, deeper waters.

1 ounce / 30 ml añejo rum

1 ounce / 30 ml Grand Marnier

½ ounce / 15 ml dry vermouth

½ ounce / 15 ml sweet vermouth

Dash grenadine

Garnish: Pared orange peel

Chill the glass. Combine the ingredients with ice in a mixing glass and stir with a barspoon for 30 seconds. Strain the cocktail into the glass. Place the orange peel on the rim and serve.

THE CANDIDATE

If the Hail to the Chief is an El Presidente riff to sip slowly and appreciate while pondering by the fireplace in your executive study, the Candidate is one to take long, thirsty swallows of when the summer heat, rather than geopolitics, has you sweating. Spreading out the rum and vermouth through pomegranate juice and seltzer—without adding sugar—makes this low-ABV, Spritz (page 100)–adjacent cooler perfect for the pool and porch.

1 ounce / 30 ml pomegranate juice

1 ounce / 30 ml white rum

¾ ounce / 22 ml dry Curaçao

¾ ounce / 22 ml dry vermouth

4 drops rose water

Seltzer to top, about 2 ounces / 60 ml

Garnish: Pomegranate seeds, orange wheel

Fill the glass with the ice. Add all the ingredients except the seltzer to a Boston shaker with ice and vigorously shake for 10 seconds. Strain the cocktail into the glass and stir with a barspoon for 5 seconds so the ice settles into the liquid. Top with seltzer and carefully spoon some pomegranate seeds on top so they float on the surface. Garnish with an orange wheel and serve.

◀ Hail to the Chief, The Candidate, Running Mates

RUNNING MATES

Frozen, overflowing a hollowed-out pineapple, and festooned with two straws for sharing, the Running Mates looks like happy hour at the Hilton Hawaiian Village, but its appearance disguises restrained sweetness and unexpected spirits. Sure, rum is a given in frozen cocktails, but when was the last time you saw El Presidente's other modifiers, Curaçao and vermouth, given the blended treatment? The result is as delightful for its taste as it is for how it subverts expectations.

This riff calls for Stiggins' Fancy Pineapple Rum and Pierre Ferrand Dry Curaçao, both of which are collaborations between master blender and Maison Ferrand founder Alexandre Gabriel and David Wondrich. While you can substitute another dry Curaçao with fine results, the pineapple rum is essential. Named for the Dickens character Reverend Stiggins, a lover of pineapple rum, the collaboration is a delectable blending of Ferrand's 3 Stars white rum redistilled with pineapple rinds and Original Dark rum infused with pineapple fruit. In addition to the Running Mates, it's excellent in the Horchatai (page 152) and the Bonfire of the Daiquiris (page 111).

1 large pineapple

3 ounces / 90 ml Plantation Stiggins' Fancy Pineapple Rum

¾ ounce / 22 ml Pierre Ferrand Dry Curaçao

¾ ounce / 22 ml dry vermouth

½ ounce / 15 ml orange juice

¼ ounce / 7 ml strained lime juice

¼ ounce / 7 ml grenadine

12 ounces / 340 g ice, about 3 cups

Garnish: Bendy straw x 2

Slice off and discard the crown of the pineapple. Carefully remove about two-thirds of the fruit and core; it should be enough to approximately fill a 1 quart/1 L container. Reserve the hollowed pineapple for serving. Juice and strain the quart of fruit. Measure out 1 ounce/30 ml of juice and add it to a blender with the remaining ingredients. Blend the mixture until smooth and frosty. Place the pitcher in the freezer for 15 minutes to set the texture, then pour the cocktail into the hollowed pineapple, using a spoon to help if needed. Garnish with the straws and enjoy with a friend.

WORKSHOP: GRENADINE

First impressions endure, which is why so many people associate grenadine with a phosphorescent red waterfall poured from a bar caddy of cocktail cherries into a fizzy cup of cola, lemon-lime soda, or ginger ale. Shirley Temples and jury-rigged Cherry Cokes have powered generations of kids' tables, but the real grenadine is nothing like what that bored bartender streamed into plastic pitchers of pop at your cousin's bar mitzvah in 1991.

Real grenadine isn't cherry-flavored, but pomegranate-flavored. The word itself is derived from the Spanish for pomegranate. The vermilion syrup has shown up in cocktails since the mid-1800s, perhaps the most popular of which is the Jack Rose, the grenadine-sweetened applejack classic shouted out in Hemingway's *The Sun Also Rises*. Imitators, meanwhile, have been around since at least 1912, when the federal government argued in *U.S. v. Thirty Cases Purporting to be Grenadine Syrup* that manufacturers were hoodwinking consumers with "grenadine" made from fruits other than pomegranate. They lost the case, opening the door to more than a century of legally sanctioned grenadine knockoffs.

While quality bottled brands (Jack Rudy, BG Reynolds) have become available in recent years, making your own is as simple as making any other cocktail syrup. It takes just four ingredients: equal measures of pomegranate juice and sugar, a shot of lemon for acidity and improved shelf-life, and orange blossom water, which adds dimension of flavor along with a lovely fragrance. (Rose water works well, too.) In addition to sweetening cocktails and nonalcoholic beverages like lemonade and seltzer, this grenadine is fantastic drizzled over vanilla ice cream, Greek yogurt, and fresh berries.

MAKES ABOUT 1 CUP / 236 ML

½ cup / 118 ml pomegranate juice

½ cup / 100 g granulated sugar

1 dash orange blossom water

½ ounce / 15 ml strained lemon juice

Equipment: Saucepot, 1 quart/1 L airtight container

Bring the pomegranate juice to a boil in a small saucepot over medium-high heat, then slowly add the sugar. Stir to completely dissolve. Allow the pomegranate mixture to return to a boil, reduce the heat to medium, and gently boil for 5 minutes. Carefully remove the pot from the heat, stir in the orange blossom water, and allow the grenadine to completely cool. Stir in the lemon juice. Transfer the finished grenadine to an airtight container and store in the refrigerator, where it will keep for 1 month.

RED RUM FIZZ

MAKES 1 COCKTAIL

GLASS: COLLINS
ICE: STANDARD CUBES

1½ ounces / 45 ml white rum

½ ounce / 15 ml grenadine

½ ounce / 15 ml strained blood orange juice

Seltzer to top, about 2 ounces / 60 ml

Garnish: Blood orange wheel

Fill the glass with the ice. Add the rum, grenadine, and blood orange juice to a Boston shaker with ice and vigorously shake for 15 seconds. Strain the cocktail into the glass and top with the seltzer. Garnish with a blood orange wheel and serve.

Step 1

Step 2

Step 3

Step 4

GRASSHOPPER

MAKES 1 COCKTAIL

GLASS: COUPE | ICE: NONE

1 ounce / 30 ml green crème de menthe

1 ounce / 30 ml white crème de cacao

1 ounce / 30 ml heavy cream

Garnish: Expressed spearmint leaf

Combine the ingredients in a Boston shaker with ice and vigorously shake for 20 seconds. Strain the cocktail into the glass. Float the expressed leaf on the surface and serve.

In 1918 or 1919—there's some uncertainty over when exactly—Philip or Philibert Guichet—there's some uncertainty over who exactly—invented the Grasshopper. Guichet was the owner or the son of the owner—there's some uncertainty over which exactly—of Tujague's, a New Orleans establishment founded in 1856 and still in operation in the French Quarter. Cocktail lore is full of these uncertainties, especially pre-Prohibition, but we do know Guichet's creamed elixir of crèmes de menthe and cacao earned honored status at Tujague's, where more than 100 years later, customers come for Grasshoppers graced with brandy floats.

The creamless category of *crème* liqueurs appears early in written cocktail history. Jerry Thomas's 1862 *The Bartenders Guide* has 22 recipes, including obscure potions like crèmes de Martinique (vanilla, neroli, roses, and cinnamon) and imperiale (carrot seed, angelica, cinnamon, and orris root), as well as the familiar cacao and menthe still used in bars today. These bottles reached the zenith of their popularity in the 1950s–70s in cocktails like the Brandy Alexander (page 156) and Pink Squirrel, which—along with a blended, milkshake-y take on the Grasshopper— were fixtures of the Wisconsin supper club scene.

"The combination of the state's appreciation for ice cream, aggressive marketing efforts by local dairy councils, and the convivial supper club atmosphere likely combined to develop Wisconsinites' taste for the sweet cocktail," *Eater*'s Erin DeJesus wrote in 2014. "While brandy Old Fashioneds are still considered a pre-meal drink, Grasshoppers . . . are served more as an after-dinner treat."

The Grasshopper is having a bit of a moment, as contemporary bartenders have been introducing fresh mint and amari to blunt the sweetness of this mint-chocolaty frappé. For that sort of take, see our Virgil's Grasshopper riff on the next page, but the original formula still holds up as a peerless liquid dessert, with or without ice cream.

GRASSHOP LIKE A WISCONSINITE

Substitute the heavy cream with two scoops of vanilla ice cream, process in a blender or milkshake machine, and serve in a chilled sundae glass.

VIRGIL'S GRASSHOPPER

MAKES 1 COCKTAIL
GLASS: COUPE | ICE: NONE

Sweet, creamy, and rich, the classic three-part Grasshopper definitely drinks like dessert. This riff updates the cocktail for modern palates. It's a little bitter, a little sweet, and benefits from fresh muddled mint. If you can't find peppermint and spearmint, using one or the other will still create a delicious and refreshing drink. The Tempus Fugit brand of crèmes de menthe and cacao, however, are nonnegotiable for this version. The California-based restorer of historic liqueurs crafts its crèmes to be more complex and less sugary than commercial counterparts. The name refers to the Latin for "time flies," a phrase coined by the poet Virgil, who lends this Grasshopper his name.

12 large spearmint leaves

12 large peppermint leaves

1 ounce / 30 ml heavy cream

1¼ ounce / 37 ml Tempus Fugit Crème de Cacao

¾ ounce / 22 ml Tempus Fugit Crème de Menthe Glaciale

Garnish: Grated dark chocolate

Chill the glass. Combine the mints and cream in a Boston shaker and vigorously muddle. Add ice and the remaining ingredients and vigorously shake for 20 seconds. Strain the cocktail into the glass, grate the chocolate over the surface, and serve.

MEADOW JUMPER

MAKES 1 COCKTAIL
GLASS: COUPE | ICE: NONE

The Meadow Jumper strips the Grasshopper and sells it for parts. From the classic formula, only the crème de cacao remains in this riff. It contains no dairy, instead using powdered lactic acid dissolved into apple juice to create the tangy illusion of crème fraîche or yogurt on the palate without giving weight to the cocktail—kind of like the opposite maneuver of a Clarified Milk Punch (page 39). It contains no crème de menthe. The mint comes from Braulio amaro, a sweet and bitter digestivo from the Italian Alps with a whipcrack menthol-pine personality—more mint-adjacent than the straightforward Andes candy vibe of the classic. Stirred and served up, the Meadow Jumper looks completely different from and has a more complicated taste than the Grasshopper while maintaining its mint-chocolate core.

1 ounce / 30 ml white crème de cacao

1 ounce / 30 ml Braulio amaro

1 ounce / 30 ml Lactic Acid Apple Juice

Garnish: Expressed spearmint leaf

Chill the glass. Combine the ingredients with ice in a mixing glass and stir with a barspoon for 30 seconds. Strain the cocktail into the glass. Float the expressed mint on the surface and serve.

LACTIC ACID APPLE JUICE

MAKES ½ CUP / 118 ML

½ cup / 118 ml bottled or fresh, well-strained apple juice

1 teaspoon lactic acid

Combine the ingredients in an airtight container and gently shake to dissolve the acid. Store in the refrigerator, where it will keep 2 weeks if made with bottled juice or 3 days if made with fresh.

◀ Virgil's Grasshopper, Meadow Jumper, Franklin Mint

FRANKLIN MINT

MAKES 1 COCKTAIL

GLASS: COLLINS | ICE: STANDARD CUBES

Looking for a session-able Grasshopper-style cocktail? Invest in the Franklin Mint. Served over ice in a Collins glass, this cocktail spreads the alcoholic crèmes de menthe and cacao across a healthy pour of milk tea—think bubble tea, minus the boba—steeped with plenty of fresh mint. The Minted Mint Tea would also be terrific with Bourbon as a creamy take on the Mint Julep (page 31).

¾ ounce / 22 ml green crème de menthe

¾ ounce / 22 ml white crème de cacao

4 ounces / 118 ml Minted Milk Tea, chilled

Garnish: Expressed spearmint sprig, metal straw

Combine the ingredients in order in the glass with the ice. (The crème de menthe will sink to the bottom.) Top with more ice if needed, garnish with the expressed mint and straw, and serve. Stir before drinking.

MINTED MILK TEA

MAKES ABOUT 6 CUPS / 1.4 L

4 cups / 1L water, divided

1½ loosely packed cups spearmint, roughly chopped

2 tablespoons loose black tea

¼ cup / 50 g brown sugar

¾ cup / 177 ml sweetened condensed milk

Bring half of the water to a boil in a saucepot over medium-high heat. Remove from heat and add the mint and tea. Steep for 5 minutes, then carefully strain off and discard the mint and tea, returning the liquid to the pot. Add the brown sugar, stirring to completely dissolve. Add the condensed milk and remaining water, stirring to combine. Transfer the finished tea to an airtight container and store in the refrigerator, where it will keep for 1 week.

It's a sweet, green miracle.

—RAJ KOOTHRAPPALI,
  "THE GRASSHOPPER EXPERIMENT," *THE BIG BANG THEORY*

WORKSHOP:
ISI WHIP

———————

You know the thick, stiff turrets of whipped cream that top photogenic banana splits and sundaes at discriminating ice cream parlors? You don't get those defined snowy peaks from a can but from an iSi Whip, the Xerox of the cream whipper world. It consists of a canister (typically stainless steel) and a screw-on lid with a chamber for small NO_2 (nitrous oxide) cartridge and a spout for dispensing. Charging the cream inside the canister with the NO_2 transforms it from a liquid state to an aerated but stable consistency.

The same principle applies to cream-based cocktails, like the Grasshopper. While you can run pretty much any liquid through an iSi Whip, it would turn something like a Martini (page 92) or Manhattan (page 84) into foamy bubbles. Dairy, on the other hand, is a favorable environment for the NO_2 to do its thing, like a slack balloon waiting to be inflated.

Given the forethought required to iSi Whip a cocktail—you need to prep and chill the mixture ahead of time, and keep the carafe cold until serving—it makes the most sense to make a batch. Most models of whippers have 1 quart/1 L carafes, so you want a max of 2 cups/470 ml of liquid to account for the increased volume from the aeration. Our Whipped Grasshopper makes about four cocktails. Try dispensing them into sundae glasses or wide Champagne coupes to emphasize their mousse-like texture.

WHIPPED GRASSHOPPER

ACTIVE TIME: 5 MINUTES | TOTAL PROJECT TIME: 1 HOUR

MAKES ABOUT 4 COCKTAILS

GLASS: COUPE X 4 | ICE: NONE

5 ounces / 148 ml green crème
de menthe

5 ounces / 148 ml white crème
de cacao

5 ounces / 148 ml heavy cream

Garnish: Grated dark chocolate,
Luxardo or Brandied Cherry (page 90)
x 4, demitasse spoons x 4

Equipment: 1 quart/1 L cream whipper,
such as iSi brand, with 1 NO_2 cartridge

Combine the ingredients in the canister
of a cream whipper. Screw on the lid
and shake to mix. Place the whipper in
the fridge along with the glasses and
chill for at least 1 hour. When ready to
serve, chill the glasses and screw the
NO_2 cartridge onto the cream whipper.
Vigorously shake the whipper. Carefully
dispense the cocktail into the glasses.
Garnish each drink with grated chocolate and a cherry and serve with
a spoon.

Step 1

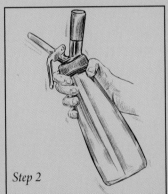

Step 2

Step 3

OTHER COCKTAILS TO WHIP:

HORCHATAI (page 152)

PIÑA COQUITO (page 178)

FRENCH 75

1 ounce / 30 ml London Dry gin

½ ounce / 15 ml strained lemon juice

½ ounce / 15 ml Simple Syrup (page 4)

Chilled Champagne to top, about 2 ounces / 60 ml

Garnish: Spiral lemon peel

Chill the glass. Combine the gin, lemon, and syrup in a Boston shaker with ice and vigorously shake for 30 seconds. Strain the cocktail into the glass and top with Champagne. Twist the peel to express the oils, drop it in the cocktail, and serve.

Its official name was the *canon de 75 modèle 1897,* but on the World War I battlefield, American GIs simply referred to the field gun as the French 75. The weapon's powerful hydraulic recoil gave it quite a kick, which is how a strong Champagne cocktail bouncing around Europe and North America since at least the 1860s eventually took the gun's name as its own several decades later.

David Wondrich references Charles Dickens, who, while visiting Boston in 1867, "liked to entertain the literary lions of the town in his room at the Parker House with 'Tom gin and champagne cups,' as an 1885 article about the hotel claimed. A Champagne Cup is bubbly, sugar, citrus and ice. Add Tom gin, as that story seems to indicate, and you've got something perilously close to the French 75."

Potent but elegant, the mixture of sweetened gin, lemon, and Champagne first appeared in print under the name French 75 in *Here's How!,* a Prohibition-era pocket manual from 1927, nine years after the Allied victory, by a bartender credited only as Judge Jr. "This drink is really what won the War for Allies," reads the note above the recipe. The formula in the seminal *Savoy Cocktail Book* from 1930 offers the cautionary coda, "Hits with remarkable precision."

BRIT 75

A dignified English accent on the French 75. The gin, lemon, and Champagne remain, while Simple Syrup trades places with a homemade Earl Grey Syrup. This not only sweetens the cocktail but also infuses it with gentle tannins and the bergamot citrus essence that's quintessential to British teatime.

1 ounce / 30 ml London Dry gin

¾ ounce / 22 ml strained lemon juice

¾ ounce / 22 ml Earl Grey Syrup

Chilled Champagne to top, about 2 ounces / 60 ml

Garnish: Pared orange peel

Chill the glass. Combine the gin, lemon, and syrup in a Boston shaker with ice and vigorously shake for 30 seconds. Strain the cocktail into the glass and top with Champagne. Place the orange peel on the rim and serve.

EARL GREY SYRUP

MAKES ABOUT 1½ CUPS / 350 ML

2 Earl Grey tea bags

1 cup / 236 ml water

1 cup / 200 g granulated sugar

Bring the water to a boil in a small pot over medium-high heat. Add the tea bags, cover, and remove from heat. Steep for 5 minutes. Remove the tea bags and add the sugar. Place over low heat and stir to dissolve. Transfer the finished syrup to an airtight container and store in the refrigerator, where it will keep for 2 weeks.

SUMMER 75

MAKES 1 COCKTAIL

GLASS: RED WINE | ICE: LARGE CUBE X 4

Bubbly, citrusy, fairly sweet, and served in the Spritz (page 100) style in a wine goblet with lots of ice, the Summer 75 is built for warm, languorous evenings in the yard and on the porch. Genever, gin's Dutch granddaddy, is less bracing than its offspring and moves with the same rhythm as honey and Meyer lemon juice, each ingredient mellower than its familiar. Lemon verbena, muddled into the cocktail and added as a garnish, lends an ephemeral green-meets-candied citrus quality. If you can't find fresh, add 2 tablespoons dried (widely available at tea shops and online) to the boiling water in the Honey Syrup recipe to make a tea, then strain, and proceed with adding the honey.

2 lemon verbena sprigs

¾ ounce / 22 ml strained Meyer lemon juice

1½ ounce / 45 ml genever

¾ ounce / 22 ml Honey Syrup (page 4)

Chilled Champagne to top, about 2 ounces / 60 ml

Garnish: Expressed Meyer lemon peel, lemon verbena sprig

Set up the glass with the ice. Combine the verbena and lemon juice in a Boston shaker and vigorously muddle. Add the genever, syrup, and ice and vigorously shake for 30 seconds. Strain the cocktail into the glass and top with Champagne. Express the lemon peel over the surface of the drink, rub it around the rim, and drop it in the cocktail. Garnish with a sprig of lemon verbena and serve.

BOTTLE ROCKET

Like the Solera Negroni (page 56), the Bottle Rocket is a batched cocktail. This recipe yields half a dozen drinks that you blend in a pitcher, bottle in advance, and chill before serving, which makes it perfect for entertaining. Instead of gin, this 75 uses Bourbon fortified with apple butter, which also fills in as the sweetener for the usual Simple Syrup and lends the drink an early autumn vibe. The Bottle Rockets will hold their bubble for about an hour in the bottles. If you want to make them further in advance, leave the Champagne out, and add it right before serving.

1 cup / 236 ml Bourbon

¼ cup / 60 ml apple butter

3¾ ounces / 111 ml strained lemon juice

4 ounces / 118 ml cold water

Chilled Champagne to top, about 3 cups / 710 ml

Garnish: Metal straw x 6

Set up the bottles. Combine the Bourbon and apple butter in a pitcher and vigorously stir to incorporate. When the butter is completely melted into the Bourbon, add the lemon and water, and stir to combine. Using a funnel, evenly divide the mixture between the bottles, about 2 ounces/60 ml each. Evenly top with Champagne. Close the bottles and chill for at least 30 minutes and up to 1 hour. Before serving, gently turn each bottle upside down to break up any settling. Open the bottles, garnish each with a metal straw, and serve.

Brit 75, Summer 75, Bottle Rocket ▶

THE COGNAC QUESTION

Some experts, like the folks at Arnaud's French 75 Bar in New Orleans, insist a proper French 75 is made with Cognac, not gin. While this is a 20th-century phenomenon, there is some evidence of French brandy appearing in the early, grenadine-blushed 75 formulas, like the ones in 1922's *Cocktails—How to Mix Them* and the 1923 edition of *Harry's ABCs of Mixing Cocktails,* both of which call for a blend of gin and Calvados. Speaking to *Punch* in 2018, Joaquín Simó of Alchemy Consulting and New York's Pouring Ribbons, offered a compromise: "It's a seasonal drink. In the spring and summer, I want it with gin. In the fall and winter, I want it with Cognac." To make the modern brandy version: Replace all the gin with Cognac. To make the 1920s version: Replace ⅔ ounce/20 ml of the gin with Calvados and replace the Simple Syrup with grenadine.

WORKSHOP:
SMOKED GLASSWARE

Smoking glasses became a trendy bar trick in the 2010s, but when used properly, the technique can truly complement a cocktail's flavor—and there's no denying the razzle-dazzle factor of glasses aswirl in fragrant, billowing plumes. While there are handheld culinary smoking guns on the market expressly designed for this purpose, you don't need 'em. To smoke your glasses, all you need is a small torch, like the kind you'd use to caramelize sugar on crème brûlée, wood chips, and a fireproof surface. Hickory and oak are good all-purpose suggestions—they go with everything and are widely available in chip form—but you can also experiment with other woods like cherry, birch, cedar, and apple or apply this method to a branch of rosemary to introduce an herbal note to the smokiness.

TOTAL PROJECT TIME: 5 MINUTES

Equipment: Small handheld torch, 1 small wood chip of choice, 1 glass of choice

Place the wood chip on a fireproof surface. Use the torch to carefully light the chip on fire. As soon as it starts to burn, cover the entire chip with the glass. Deprived of oxygen, the flame will snuff out quickly and the smoke will season the inside of the glass. Leave the glass upside down until ready to serve.

Step 1

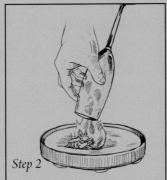

Step 2

Step 3

HARRY'S SMOKED 75

The French 75 is such a celebratory cocktail, and a smoked flute really levels up the presentation. We particularly like applying the technique to the drink's circa-1923 Calvados-and-gin formula from Harry's ABCs of Mixing Cocktails. The oak-smoked glass makes a nice callback to the French apple brandy, which is aged in oak barrels.

MAKES 1 COCKTAIL
GLASS: SMOKED CHAMPAGNE
FLUTE | ICE: NONE

⅔ ounce / 20 ml Calvados

⅓ ounce / 10 ml London Dry gin

2 dashes absinthe

1 teaspoon grenadine

Chilled Champagne to top,
about 2 ounces / 60 ml

Garnish: Luxardo or Bourbon
Cherry (page 90)

Combine the Calvados, gin, absinthe, and grenadine in a Boston shaker with ice and vigorously shake for 30 seconds. Drop the cherry into the bottom of the prepared glass. Strain the cocktail into the glass, top with Champagne, and serve.

OTHER COCKTAILS TO
SERVE IN SMOKED GLASSES:

MARGARITA (page 164)

NAKED AND FAMOUS (page 190)

WHISKEY SOUR (page 76)

MAI TAI

MAKES 1 COCKTAIL
GLASS: ROCKS | ICE: CRUSHED OR PEBBLE

1½ ounces / 45 ml white rum

½ ounce / 15 ml strained lime juice

½ ounce / 15 ml dry Curaçao

½ ounce / 15 ml orgeat

Garnish: Lime wheel, spearmint sprig

Combine the ingredients in a Boston shaker with ice and vigorously shake for 20 seconds. Pack the glass with the ice. Strain the cocktail over the ice and mound more ice on top. Garnish with a lime wheel and a mint sprig and serve.

"Anyone who says I didn't create this drink is a dirty stinker," tiki impresario Victor J. Bergeron wrote in his 1972 *Trader Vic's Bartender's Guide.* In his origin story of the Mai Tai, he presented the shaken mix of rum, lime, orange liqueur, orgeat, and Simple Syrup to some Tahitian friends, who declared the frothy cocktail *"Maita'i roa a'e!"* or "Out of this world! The best!"

The "dirty stinker" challenging Bergeron's claim was Donn "the Beachcomber" Beach. There's no argument that Beach's tiki bar, Don the Beachcomber, arrived on the scene first, opening in Hollywood in 1933. (Bergeron's first Trader Vic's, originally called Hinky Dinks, opened in San Francisco the following year.) Beach argued Bergeron cribbed the Mai Tai formula from his Q.B. Cooler, another rum drink involving several syrups and juices, and while Bergeron won the legal rights to the name Mai Tai, the entrepreneurs remained good-natured rivals as their respective restaurants appropriated Polynesian culture and shipped it from the South Pacific to the US mainland throughout the 1940s and beyond.

Time and greed were unkind to the Mai Tai, as they have been to many other tropical cocktails. Like the Piña Colada (page 174), Margarita (page 164), and Daiquiri (page 108), the Mai Tai devolved into a sweet, fruity confection, a bottled mix, and a punch line, only to be rescued, stripped to the studs, and restored to status in the early 2000s. When made the classic way, the Mai Tai is magic, the rum swooning through waves of citrus and sweet almonds.

Speaking of almonds, orgeat is a common almond-based elixir in tiki cocktails. You pronounce it "OR-zhat" and can either make your own—see the workshop at the end of this chapter—or use a high-quality bottled version from brands like BG Reynolds.

WHITE LIE

MAKES 1 COCKTAIL
GLASS: COUPE | ICE: NONE

Turning the Mai Tai into the White Lie requires two quick substitutions. The bright Brazilian sugarcane spirit cachaça (most commonly used in the Caipirinha cocktail that rode the Mojito's coattails to popularity in the United States) replaces rum, and almond milk replaces the orgeat, creating a drier cocktail with the acidic thwack of a Daiquiri (page 108) or Gimlet (page 42). The expressed basil leaf garnish reaches up and drags you into this drink by the nose.

1½ ounces / 45 ml cachaça

½ ounce / 15 ml strained lime juice

½ ounce / 15 ml dry Curaçao

½ ounce / 15 ml unsweetened almond milk

Garnish: Expressed basil leaf

Chill the glass. Combine the ingredients in a Boston shaker with ice and vigorously shake for 15 seconds. Strain the cocktail into the glass. Float the expressed basil on the drink and serve.

MANGO MAI TAI

MAKES 1 COCKTAIL

GLASS: PINT | ICE: CRUSHED OR PEBBLE

Did you ever have a traumatizing encounter with Captain Morgan in college? Same. But don't be nervous about this spiced rum–based Mai Tai. High-quality bottles with nuanced spice profiles, like Bumbu and Sailor Jerry, are helping to redeem the black sheep of the rum family, and this is a perfect cocktail for a reintroduction. The Mango Mai Tai's main twist on the classic is its infusion of the titular fruit into the spiced rum. That functions as the base of the recipe, which proceeds in usual Mai Tai format with Curaçao, orgeat, and lime.

1½ ounces / 45 ml Spiced Mango Rum

½ ounce / 15 ml dry Curaçao

½ ounce / 15 ml orgeat

½ ounce / 15 ml strained lime juice

Garnish: Spearmint sprig, mango spear

Combine ingredients in a Boston shaker with ice and vigorously shake for 20 seconds. Pack the glass with the ice. Strain the cocktail over the ice and mound more ice on top. Garnish with the mint and mango and serve.

SPICED MANGO RUM

MAKES 1½ CUPS / 350 ML

1½ cups / 350 ml spiced rum

1 cup / 160 g dried mango, roughly chopped

Combine the ingredients in an airtight container and vigorously shake for 5 seconds. Allow to infuse in a cool, dark place for 3 days, vigorously shaking once a day. Taste the infusion after 3 days. If the mango flavor isn't very pronounced—this will depend on the quality of the dried mango—continue to infuse and taste once a day until desired flavor is achieved.

◀ White Lie, Mango Mai Tai, Horchatai

HORCHATAI

MAKES 1 COCKTAIL

GLASS: 8 OUNCE/236 ML MILK BOTTLE | ICE: CRUSHED OR PEBBLE

Perfumed with cinnamon, sweet, and creamy, horchata is a rice-milk beverage popular in Mexico and other parts of Latin America. Our recipe uses almonds as well as rice, allowing horchata to fill the orgeat role in this Mai Tai riff. The Horchatai is an ideal recipe for batching into bottles like the Solera Negroni (page 56) and Bottle Rocket (page 144), so consider scaling up. You can also drink the extra horchata on its own, though note that this recipe makes a drier version than normal since it's being used in a cocktail rather than consumed solo. To make horchata for stand-alone drinking, add 1 cup/200 g granulated sugar to the mixture.

2 ounces / 60 ml chilled Horchata

1½ ounces / 45 ml rhum agricole

½ ounce / 15 ml dry Curaçao

¼ ounce / 7 ml strained lime juice

Garnish: Grated cinnamon, Cinnamon Incense (page 197), metal straw

Fill the bottle with ice. Combine the ingredients in a Boston shaker with ice and vigorously shake for 20 seconds. Strain the cocktail into the bottle and dust the surface with Cinnamon Incense. Lay Cinnamon Incense across the rim of the bottle and serve.

HORCHATA

MAKES ABOUT 1 QUART / 1 L

2 cups / 370 g long-grain white rice

5 cups / 1.2 L water

7 ounces (½ can) sweetened condensed milk

¼ cup / 72 g almonds, toasted

2 cinnamon sticks, lightly toasted

¼ teaspoon vanilla extract

Combine all the ingredients in a large airtight container, ceramic pot, or mixing bowl, cover, and allow to soak for at least 8 hours at room temperature. Transfer the mixture to a blender and puree until very smooth. Filter the mixture through a strainer lined with cheesecloth. Transfer the horchata to an airtight container and store in the refrigerator, where it will keep for 10 days.

WORKSHOP:
ORGEAT

O rgeat syrup became a popular cocktail ingredient during the tiki era of the 1930s and '40s, but its existence far predates that time. It's thought that orgeat was first based not on nuts, but rather grains; *orge* is French for barley, and the original drink would have been something akin to a nondairy milk. To improve its bland flavor, people began adding sugar, orange blossom or rose water, and bitter almond, which has a lovely marzipan aroma and potentially toxic levels of cyanide. Contemporary historians have speculated that orgeat even played a role in the assassination of Napoleon.

Don't worry; nobody is making orgeat with bitter almonds now. If you see "bitter almond" on an ingredient list, it's just the industry sobriquet for bitter almond oil, which is extracted from the pits of stone fruits like apricots, cherries, and peaches. But why even bother with the confusion, especially when homemade orgeat is extremely easy to put together? The process consists of grinding almonds into a fine powder, making Simple Syrup, boiling those things together, and stirring in orange blossom water for flavor and brandy for preservation. It's supersimple.

Once you have a bottle of orgeat at the ready in your fridge, don't limit yourself to just using it in Mai Tais and other cocktails, like the Elba Fizz (below). Around the world, people mix it with seltzer and citrus for a refreshing nonalcoholic drink. It turns lemonade cloudy and nutty-sweet, can punch up ice cream and sorbet bases, and is delicious drizzled over Greek yogurt.

MAKES ABOUT 1¹/₂ CUPS / 350 ML

1½ cups / 214 g raw almonds

1 cup / 236 ml water

1 cup / 200 g granulated sugar

1 ounce / 30 ml brandy

¼ teaspoon orange blossom water

Equipment: Food processor, saucepot, 1 quart/1 L airtight container

Grind the almonds to a fine consistency in a food processor or blender and set aside. Bring the water to a boil in a small saucepot on the stove. Add the sugar and stir to completely dissolve. When the mixture returns to a boil, stir in the ground almonds. Let the mixture boil again, then reduce the heat and allow to cook at a low boil for 5 minutes. Carefully remove the pot from the heat, stir in the brandy and orange blossom water, and allow to completely cool. Transfer the finished orgeat to an airtight container and store in the refrigerator, where it will keep for 1 month.

THE COCKTAIL WORKSHOP

ELBA FIZZ

MAKES 1 COCKTAIL
GLASS: COLLINS
ICE: STANDARD CUBES

1½ ounces / 45 ml white rum

1 ounce / 30 ml orgeat

San Pellegrino Limonata to top, about 3 ounces / 90 ml

Garnish: Lemon wheel

Fill the glass with the ice. Add all the rum and orgeat to a Boston shaker with ice and vigorously shake for 15 seconds. Strain the cocktail into the glass, top with the Limonata, and gently stir with a barspoon to combine. Garnish with the lemon and serve.

Step 1

Step 2

Step 3

Step 4

Step 5

OTHER ORGEAT
COMBINATIONS TO TRY:

Cashew + coconut flavoring

Hazelnut + vanilla extract

Pistachio + rose water

BRANDY ALEXANDER

MAKES 1 COCKTAIL
GLASS: COUPE | ICE: NONE

1 ounce / 30 ml Cognac

1 ounce / 30 ml crème dark de cacao

1 ounce / 30 ml heavy cream

Garnish: Grated nutmeg

Chill the glass. Combine the ingredients in a Boston shaker with ice and vigorously shake for 30 seconds. Strain the cocktail into the glass. Grate the nutmeg over the surface and serve.

In the fall of 1915, the Philadelphia Phillies and the Boston Red Sox faced off in the World Series with Triple Crown–winning pitcher (and future Hall of Famer) Grover Cleveland "Pete" Alexander on the mound for the Phillies in Game 1. The week prior to the start of the championship, the *Philadelphia Inquirer* had run a story about the hubbub percolating in the city, noting, "The head bartender" at the Philadelphia Racquet Club "has even gone so far as to invent an Alexander cocktail, which he is reserving to be served during the World Series." It's widely assumed the drink was named for the right-handed ace, who would go on to win that Game 1, allowing just one earned run.

From that World Series—the Phillies lost—and through the repeal of Prohibition, it seems the Alexander came to represent a family of cocktails in which the primary spirit could be swapped in based on the drinker's preference. Both gin and brandy versions appear in 1937 cocktail guides, *New Orleans Drinks and How to Mix 'em* and *Café Royal Cocktail Book,* respectively, but the latter version would come to dominate in the United States in subsequent decades, eventually becoming tightly associated with Midwest supper clubs, particularly in Wisconsin, where it's often made with vanilla ice cream like its after-dinner partner, the Grasshopper (page 132).

BRANDY LEBOWSKI

MAKES 1 COCKTAIL

GLASS: HIGHBALL | ICE: LARGE CUBE X 5

This easy tweak on the Brandy Alexander reformats the drink in the proportions of a White Russian, where brandy steps in for the usual vodka. (If you don't get the name, go rent The Big Lebowski.) Kahlua is the most readily available coffee liqueur, but you can also substitute an equal measurement of our homemade version from the Cold Brew Old Fashioned (page 72).

2 ounces / 60 ml American brandy

1 ounce / 30 ml Kahlua or Coffee Liqueur (page 72)

1½ ounce / 45 ml heavy cream

Garnish: Grated nutmeg

Fill the glass with the ice. Combine the ingredients in a Boston shaker with ice and vigorously shake for 30 seconds. Strain the cocktail into the glass and add ice if necessary. Grate the nutmeg over the surface and serve.

◄ Brandy Lebowski, Armie Alexander, Brandy Alexander Flip

ARMIE ALEXANDER

Like its better-known cousin, Cognac, Armagnac is a French fruit brandy aged in oak barrels, but there are a couple differences, namely that Armagnac is made from a blend of grapes and column-distilled once before aging, whereas Cognac is primarily Ugni Blanc and pot-distilled twice. This makes Armagnac the more rambunctious of the two brandies, and though there are lots of lovely bottles for sipping, it's also a more economical mixer that can stand in a busy cocktail like this spiked chocolate-cream fizz.

¾ ounce / 22 ml Armagnac

¾ ounce / 22 ml dark crème de cacao

1 ounce / 30 ml half-and-half

Splash vanilla extract

Seltzer to top, about 1 to 2 ounces / 30–60 ml

Garnish: 2 skewered Luxardo or Brandied Cherries (page 90), metal straw

Fill the glass with the ice. Combine the Armagnac, crème de cacao, cream, and vanilla in a Boston shaker with ice and vigorously shake for 20 seconds. Strain the cocktail into the glass, add ice if necessary, and top with the seltzer. Lay the skewered cherries across the rim, garnish with the straw, and serve.

THE COCKTAIL WORKSHOP

BRANDY ALEXANDER FLIP

MAKES 1 COCKTAIL

GLASS: SNIFTER | ICE: NONE

The key to well executed whole-egg cocktails like Flips and Nogs is thorough shaking, even more so than in egg-white cocktails. It takes a full minute of iceless agitation to completely incorporate the white and yolk into the brandy, rye, oat milk, and maple syrup. The effort is worth it, producing a Flip so silky and rich it drinks like an adult milkshake.

1 ounce / 30 ml Cognac

1 ounce / 30 ml Cacao Rye

1 ounce / 30 ml oat milk

¾ ounce / 22 ml maple syrup

1 egg

Garnish: Grated nutmeg, grated cinnamon

Combine ingredients in a Boston shaker and vigorously dry-shake for 1 minute. Add ice and shake for 20 seconds to chill. Strain the cocktail into the glass, grate the nutmeg and cinnamon over the surface, and serve.

CACAO RYE

MAKES 5 OUNCES / 148 ML

2 tablespoons cocoa powder

5 ounces / 148 ml rye

Combine ingredients in an airtight container and allow to infuse for 24 hours in a cool, dark place. Strain off and discard the cacao nibs and return the infused rye to the container. This will keep indefinitely, but the cacao flavor will begin to degrade after 1 month.

WORKSHOP: POUSSE CAFÉ

In the cocktail world, *pousse café* (French for "coffee pusher") can refer to a specific drink, a specific glass in which said drink is served, or a serving technique of layering a drink's ingredients so they appear stacked in color-blocked bands. Pousse café goes way back, at least to the mid-1800s; three versions appear in Jerry Thomas's *How to Mix Drinks,* though the recipes are not the layered cocktails we're discussing here but perhaps the category's original meaning of a short after-dinner sipper served with coffee.

These days, layered cocktail sightings in the wild are rare—you've most likely encountered them in 1990s party shot form (B-52, Buttery Nipple)—and few bartenders are pushing (*pousse*-ing) to bring the trick back into vogue. But mixing drinks, especially at home, doesn't have to be so self-serious, and there's something undeniably snazzy about a pousse café–style stratified cocktail.

Pousse cafés are neither shaken nor stirred, so it's key to have all your ingredients well chilled before pouring. As when adding a finishing Float (page 196) to a cocktail, you want to slowly pour each layer over the convex back of a barspoon. You work heaviest (most dissolved sugar) to lightest (least dissolved sugar). This also typically means least alcohol to most, which is why overproof spirits like 151 rum are often used as floaters.

CHOCOLATE CHERRY ALEXANDER

MAKES 1 COCKTAIL

½ ounce grenadine, chilled

1 ounce / 30 ml white crème de cacao, chilled

1 ounce / 30 ml heavy cream, chilled

1 ounce /30 ml brandy, chilled

Equipment: Pousse café glass (a Champagne flute or larger cordial glass will also work), barspoon

Chill the glass. Pour the grenadine in the bottom. Place a barspoon upside down as close as possible to the surface of the grenadine. Gently pour the crème de cacao so it floats on top. Repeat the process with the cream, then the brandy, and serve.

Step 1

Step 2

Step 3

Step 4

MARGARITA

MAKES 1 COCKTAIL

GLASS: DOUBLE OLD FASHIONED
ICE: STANDARD CUBES

2 ounces / 60 ml blanco tequila

1 ounce / 30 ml Cointreau

1 ounce / 30 ml strained
lime juice

Garnish: Kosher salt rim,
lime wedge

Rim a glass with the salt and fill it with the ice. Combine the ingredients in a Boston shaker with ice and vigorously shake for 15 seconds. Strain the cocktail into the glass, garnish with a lime wedge, and serve.

In the realm of classic cocktails, where origin stories can turn as murky as a misplaced Mojito, having the drink you claimed to invent appear in your obituary in the paper of record makes for pretty compelling evidence. But in the case of the Margarita, Carlos (Danny) Herrera's alleged on-the-fly creation in the Tijuana restaurant Rancho La Gloria, there are more counterclaims than can be counted.

Among the most straightforward is that the Margarita evolved from the Daisy, a pre-Prohibition family of cocktails featuring a drinker's choice of spirit—similar to the Mule/Buck, Smash, and Fizz—with orange liqueur, lemon, and seltzer. The Brandy Daisy was the most popular style of Daisy since the late 1800s. Swap the brandy for tequila, lemon for lime, and lose the seltzer, and you've got a Margarita, which, OK, maybe sounds like too many modifications to prove parentage—until you translate *margarita* from Spanish. Surprise: It means "daisy." And there are references to Tequila Daisies dating back to 1936, when the *Syracuse Herald* called it the city's "newest and refreshing drink." By 1939, the *Albuquerque Journal* was describing the cocktail as "ubiquitous."

Whatever the true story of the Margarita—whether its roots lie north or south of the border, whether it was named for a flower, a picky showgirl, a German ambassador's daughter (another tale), or Margarita Cansino aka Rita Hayworth (yet another)—the cocktail's simple, three-ingredient construction and brisk, invigorating nature make it one of the most enduring and beloved from the heady days following the repeal of Prohibition. While other drinks became relics of the era, the Margarita has thrived through wars and walls and remains one of the greats.

AMARORITA

MAKES 1 COCKTAIL

GLASS: COUPE | ICE: NONE

Mexico meets Italy in this bitter-forward Margarita. With aged tequila and Nonino, a Friulian amaro heavy on the bitter oranges, standing in for blanco and Cointreau, the approach is to shift the usual Marg—in both flavor and appearance—from something bright, brisk, and clear to something dark, complex, and moody. Cutting the lime juice with orange juice reinforces the orange notes and adds just enough sweet to balance the bitter.

2 ounces / 60 ml añejo tequila

1 ounce / 30 ml Nonino amaro

½ ounce / 15 ml strained orange juice

¼ ounce / 7 ml strained lime juice

Garnish: Kosher salt rim, lime wedge

Chill the glass and rim it with the salt. Combine the ingredients with ice in a mixing glass and stir with a barspoon for 30 seconds. Strain the cocktail into the glass, garnish with a lime wedge, and serve.

MARGARITA RASPADO

In Mexico, a raspado is what we would call a snow cone in the States, from the Spanish raspar, "to scrape." But unlike the frosty American treat soaked in artificial syrups, the Latin version features fresh fruits, spices, and chamoy, the intensely sweet and sour condiment made from chiles and fruit (usually mango or plums). Here, the Margarita is remixed as a raspado with a dose of tart, floral passion fruit juice.

Now, here are too many words on passion fruit: If you live in a citrus-growing region, you can probably find fresh juice in season at a farmers' market. The next best option is ordering from Twisted Alchemy, an Illinois-based company that makes cold-pressed juices with cocktails in mind and ships nationwide. Ceres, a larger natural-foods brand, sells boxed passion fruit juice—albeit cut with pear juice—that is very good and widely available. Avoid anything labeled cocktail or nectar, which will be sweetened, likely with high-fructose corn syrup.

2 ounces / 60 ml blanco tequila

1 ounce / 30 ml strained passion fruit juice

1 ounce / 30 ml strained lime juice

½ ounce / 15 ml Cointreau

Garnish: Chamoy drizzle, sea salt

Pack the cups with ice so they have rounded domes on top. Combine the ingredients in a Boston shaker with ice and vigorously shake for 20 seconds. Slowly strain the cocktail into the cups, drizzle chamoy over top, garnish with salt, and serve.

TEQUILA 101

BLANCO: Clear agave distillate typically characterized by bright citrus and pepper notes

REPOSADO: Gently aged tequila with honeyed and dried fruit flavors from time in a barrel

AÑEJO: Thoroughly matured tequila with deep vanilla and smoke notes from significant oak influence

◀ Amarorita, Margarita Raspado, 80-Proof and Sunny

80-PROOF AND SUNNY

MAKES 1 COCKTAIL

GLASS: DOUBLE OLD FASHIONED | ICE: STANDARD CUBES

Like a vacation on a faraway island, the 80-Proof and Sunny takes some effort to arrive at. You've got to juice a cantaloupe, make a saffron salt for rimming, and steep more saffron into tequila for a 24-hour tincture. It's worth it. The honeyed and floral flavors of the precious spice and ripe melon harmonize beautifully with reposado tequila. This recipe will make more cantaloupe juice then you need, so try freezing the extra in an ice cube tray and using them to make a cantaloupe version of the watermelon-based Home Stretch (page 36).

2 ounces / 60 m reposado tequila

1 ounce 30 ml strained Cantaloupe Juice

¾ ounce / 22 ml lime juice

½ ounce / 15 ml light agave syrup

4 drops Saffron Tincture

Garnish: Saffron Salt rim

Rim the glass with the Saffron Salt and fill it with the ice. Combine the ingredients in a Boston shaker with ice and vigorously shake for 20 seconds. Strain the cocktail into the glass and serve.

CANTALOUPE JUICE

MAKES ABOUT 2 CUPS / 470 ML

1 ripe cantaloupe

Slice the cantaloupe in half and scoop out the seeds. Cut the melon into long spears, remove the rind, and process the flesh in an electric juicer. Alternatively, puree the flesh in a blender and transfer the puree to a fine-mesh strainer set over a mixing bowl. Allow the juice to strain off for about 1 hour.

SAFFRON TINCTURE

MAKES 2 OUNCES / 60 ML

2 saffron threads

2 ounces / 60 ml blanco tequila

Combine the ingredients in an airtight container and allow them to infuse at room temperature for 24 hours. Remove the saffron threads from the tincture and transfer it to a small eye-dropper bottle. Store in a cool, dark place. This will keep indefinitely, but the saffron flavor will begin to degrade after 2 months.

SAFFRON SALT

MAKES ENOUGH FOR 4 COCKTAILS

2¼ tablespoons / 40 grams Morton's kosher salt

10 saffron threads

1 teaspoon water

Pulse the ingredients in a spice grinder until the mixture achieves a rich golden color. Transfer the saffron salt to a small tray, spread it out evenly, and allow it to air-dry before use. Store in an airtight container until ready to use.

They now come in strawberry, blueberry and wine flavors, some with shaved ice and some without. But, for Carlos (Danny) Herrera, there was only one way—the original way—to make a margarita. Herrera, the creator of the margarita, died this week … of natural causes. He was 90. It was in the late 1940s, in a Tijuana roadside restaurant, that he first poured the famed drink. As Herrera told it, the margarita began as an experiment when he tried to concoct something that would quench the thirst of a beautiful young showgirl named Marjorie King. "She was allergic to everything except tequila," Herrera said in a 1991 *Times* interview. "But she couldn't take it straight, or even with the lemon and the salt. But she liked it. So I started experimenting."

—OBITUARY OF CARLOS "DANNY" HERRERA, *LA TIMES*, MAY 1992

WORKSHOP: KOMBUCHA

At the turn of the new millennium, if you asked a supermarket clerk in any US city where you could find the kombucha, you'd likely have been met with an expression of confusion. Today, you'd be directed to a shelf of a dozen brands ranging from boutique startups to lines owned by soda giants eager for a foothold in the quasi-wellness-beverage space. The history of kombucha in America is short, swift, and upward, like the incline of a launched roller coaster, but the fermented tea is an ancient drink that dates to B.C. China and traveled to Europe via Russia many centuries later during WWI.

Effervescent, sour-and-sweet kombucha has surprising utility in mixed drinks. In a Margarita, it mimics the acidity of lime juice, with the added benefit of subtle bubbles. To make kombucha at home, you need a SCOBY (symbiotic culture of bacterial and yeast), the jellyfish-looking blob that converts sweetened tea into fizzy kombucha—the same function as yeast in Yeast-Carbonated Soda (page 187). Thanks to the rise of booch home-brew hobbyists, living SCOBYs are easy to purchase online, but in a pinch you can use the dregs from the bottle of store-bought *raw* kombucha, much as you would use a bit of old yogurt to kick-start the culturing of a fresh batch. (Using both, as our recipe does, is the best way to ensure lively fermentation.) In this workshop, we're making a straight-up plain kombucha from black tea, but you can experiment with different teas and add spices and other flavorings.

On safety: Avoiding contamination is extra important when brewing kombucha at home. Make sure all equipment is completely clean and sterile before using. That includes your hands, which should be thoroughly washed before handling the SCOBY.

MAKES ABOUT 1 GALLON / 3.8 L

3½ quarts / 3.3 L water

2 tablespoons loose leaf black tea

2 cups / 400 g granulated sugar

2 cups / 470 ml starter liquid, such as store-bought plain unpasteurized kombucha

1 SCOBY

Equipment: Large lidded pot, 1 gallon/3.8 L glass brewing jar, paper towels, rubber bands, funnel, spoons, bowl, 1 quart/1 L glass jar, 16 ounce/ 470 ml glass bottles with caps x 8

Step 1

Step 2

Bring the water to a boil in a large pot on the stove and remove it from heat. Add the tea and sugar, stirring to completely dissolve. Cover the pot and allow the tea to cool to room temperature.

Strain out and discard the leaves and transfer the tea to the brewing jar. Stir in the starter liquid. Transfer the SCOBY to the jar with clean hands. Cover the jar with a paper towel and secure it with one or multiple rubber bands; it should be very secure. Store the mixture in a cool, dark place for 1 week. A white film on the surface of the liquid or SCOBY, sediment, and bubbles will eventually appear, which means the fermentation is happening. If fuzzy and/or colored (black, green, blue) mold appears, discard the batch and start over.

After 1 week, carefully remove the paper towel and rubber band(s) and test the kombucha with a freshly cleaned spoon. Do this every day until it reaches the desired balance of sweetness and acidity, using a new paper towel between tastings. Once the ideal balance of flavor is reached, remove the SCOBY with clean hands and place it in a clean bowl. (At this step you can start the process over or store the SCOBY in the glass jar and refrigerate it for later use.) Funnel the liquid into glass bottles, seal tightly, and allow to rest at room temperature overnight. Fermentation is still happening in the liquid, so this step will allow the gas that is being produced to build up, therefore carbonating the bottles. Store in the refrigerator to stop fermentation.

Step 3

Step 4

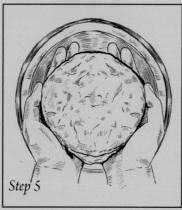

Step 5

Step 6

KOMBUCHA MARGARITA

MAKES 1 COCKTAIL
GLASS: DOUBLE OLD FASHIONED
ICE: STANDARD CUBES

2 ounces / 60 ml blanco tequila

1 ounce / 30 ml Cointreau

¾ ounce / 22 ml kombucha

½ ounce / 15 ml Simple Syrup
(page 4)

Garnish: Kosher salt rim,
expressed lime peel

Rim the glass with the salt and fill it with the ice. Combine the ingredients in a Boston shaker with ice and vigorously shake for 15 seconds. Strain the cocktail into the glass. Express the lime peel over the surface of the drink, rub it around the rim, drop it in the cocktail, and serve.

PIÑA COLADA

MAKES 1 COCKTAIL
GLASS: TIKI PINT
ICE: CRUSHED OR PEBBLE

2 ounces / 59 ml white rum

1½ ounces / 45 ml cream of coconut

1½ ounces / 45 ml strained pineapple juice

½ ounce / 15 ml strained lime juice

Garnish: Pineapple wedge, Luxardo or Bourbon Cherry (page 90)

Combine the ingredients in a Boston shaker and vigorously dry-shake for 30 seconds. Add ice to the shaker and shake for 15 seconds. Pack the glass with the ice. Strain the cocktail into the glass. Top with more crushed ice if needed. Pin the cherry to the rind of the pineapple with a plastic sword or toothpick and secure the pineapple to the rim of the glass. Serve.

In the 1950s, Puerto Rico was the place to be. Movie stars and jet-setters flocked to San Juan, where the glitzy Condado Beach strip sparkled with jangling casinos and luxury hotels. It was here the Piña Colada was invented in the midst of the 1954 coconut-cutters strike. When a bartender at the Caribe Hilton couldn't serve his rum-and-coconut milk cocktail in its usual coconut shell, he improvised with a hollowed-out pineapple.

That's one story, anyway. Others include pirates. Still others credit the agricultural professor who invented shelf-stable canned cream of coconut. And none other than the *New York Times* actually attributes the Piña Colada to *Cuba,* writing in the April 16, 1950, edition, "Drinks in the West Indies range from Martinique's famous rum punch to Cuba's Piña colada (rum, pineapple and coconut milk)." While the island of origin might be up for debate, the Piña Colada is a drink the entire Caribbean can be proud of. When made with fresh ingredients (instead of the sugary premade mixes that dominated in the 1970s and '80s), it's a lovely and balanced cocktail that, like mid-century San Juan, embodies tropical sophistication.

The classic recipe benefits from the dry-shake technique, in which ingredients are shaken together without ice to really combine them. Typically, you see this with cocktails that include eggs, but the thick, viscous cream of coconut in the Piña Colada needs that same vigorous agitation to break down and meld with the rum and fruit juices. Clean, basic white rum is traditional, but if you want a more complex profile, you can swap out or split it with aged rum or rhum agricole, which are featured in the Piña Colada riffs that follow.

PIÑA ARRIBA

MAKES 1 COCKTAIL
GLASS: COUPE | ICE: NONE

Clear, canary-yellow, and served up (or arriba *in Spanish) in a coupe, you'd never guess the Piña Colada as this cocktail's parent. It's like a Piña Colada dressed up for dinner—smart and velvety, with a more complex rum profile thanks to the addition of rhum agricole, a lighter body from coconut water, and absolutely ripping acidity. Sip it like you would a Gimlet (page 42).*

1 ounce / 30 ml white rum

1 ounce / 30 ml rhum agricole

1 ounce / 30 ml strained
pineapple juice

1 ounce / 30 ml coconut water

½ ounce / 15 ml strained lime juice

6 drops El Guapo Polynesian Kiss
tiki bitters

Garnish: Pared lime peel

Combine the ingredients with ice in a mixing glass and stir with a barspoon for 30 seconds. Strain into the coupe glass. Place the lime peel on the rim and serve.

RUM 101

WHITE: Unaged molasses distillate with light, bright, fruity esters and subtly sweet flavor profile

AÑEJO: Aged molasses distillate with more oak influence—think vanilla, toasted coconut, cinnamon, toffee—from time in a barrel

AGRICOLE: Rum made from sugarcane juice instead of molasses, resulting in an even lighter, herbaceous, grassy, citrus flavor

---

Piña Arriba, Ginger Lime Colada, Piña Coquito ▶

GINGER LIME COLADA

MAKES 1 COCKTAIL
GLASS: PINT | ICE: CRUSHED OR PEBBLE

Ginger juice and lime curd evolve the pineapple-coconut profile of the classic Piña, making this take delightfully sharp and light on its feet. You can juice your own ginger and make your own lime curd, but high-quality versions from your local juice bar and grocery will work well.

1 ounce / 30 ml white rum

1 ounce / 30 ml rhum agricole

1 ounce / 30 ml strained pineapple juice

1 ounce / 30 ml cream of coconut

1½ teaspoons lime curd

½ ounce / 15 ml cold-pressed ginger juice

Garnish: Candied ginger

Combine the ingredients in a Boston shaker and vigorously dry-shake for 30 seconds. Pack the glass with the ice. Strain the cocktail into the glass. Top with more crushed ice if needed. Garnish with candied ginger and serve.

PIÑA COQUITO

MAKES 1 COCKTAIL

GLASS: SNIFTER | ICE: CRUSHED OR PEBBLE

The Piña Coquito is a mash-up of two Caribbean classics, the Piña Colada and Coquito, the spiced Puerto Rican eggnog made with rum and coconut milk. The latter is a fixture at holiday gatherings, and like eggnog, it's as thick and comforting as a plush robe on Christmas morning. The introduction of pineapple juice and a good shake with plenty of ice helps dilute the richness, so you can have more than a cup without needing a nap. This recipe is easy to scale up for a crowd. You can bottle it or serve it in a punch bowl. Just be sure to add the nutmeg and orange to each cup right before serving; they take the drink to another level.

1 ounce / 30 ml white rum

1¾ / 52 ml coconut milk

¾ ounce / 22 ml condensed milk

½ ounce / 15 ml strained
pineapple juice

½ egg yolk

2 drops vanilla extract

**Garnish: Grated nutmeg,
grated orange zest**

Combine the ingredients with ice in a Boston shaker and vigorously dry-shake for 30 seconds. Add ice to the shaker and shake for 15 seconds. Pack the glass with the ice. Strain the cocktail into the glass. Grate the nutmeg and orange zest over the surface of the drink and serve.

WORKSHOP:
TEPACHE

In Mexico, where there's pineapple, there's tepache. Mexicans take all peels and core of the fruit and ferment them in water sweetened with unrefined sugar (piloncillo) into this golden-brown beverage. Tepache is sweet, tart, and slightly funky, like a mild kombucha with a big pineapple bouquet. It's fantastic and refreshing on its own, but adds something really special to a Piña Colada, introducing an almost savory element to the cocktail.

This tepache recipe uses brown sugar, which is easier to find than and a fair substitution for piloncillo, but it's worth seeking out Mexican cinnamon (canela) for its distinct perfume and flavor. Whole chopped fruit, as opposed to using just peels and core, speeds up the fermentation process. It takes at least 24 hours and up to three days to make tepache, depending on variables like ambient temperature and existing sugar content in the fruit. It's a living thing, and you need to keep checking it.

ACTIVE TIME: 15 MINUTES | TOTAL PROJECT TIME: 1 TO 3 DAYS

MAKES ABOUT 1 QUART / 1 L

1 medium pineapple

1 quart / 1 L water

2 cups / 400 g dark brown sugar

1 cinnamon stick, preferably Mexican, lightly toasted

Juice of 1 lime

Pinch kosher salt

Equipment: Large Dutch oven, strainer, 2 quart/1.9 L airtight container

Cut off and discard the crown of the pineapple. Leaving the peel intact, roughly chop the rest of the fruit, including the core, which should be about 1 pound/453, or about 4 cups. Reserve at room temperature.

Bring the water to boil in a large, clean Dutch oven or other enamel-coated pot with a lid. Remove the pot from the heat and add the sugar to the water, stirring to completely dissolve. Add the chopped pineapple and cinnamon. Cover the pot and move it to a cool, dark place. Allow the mixture to ferment, stirring and tasting twice a day. At first, the tepache will only taste sweet. As it ferments, you'll notice a subtly yeasty, slightly funky flavor in the background. Once that flavor appears, the tepache is ready. (It may or may not become effervescent, depending on the activity of the fermentation, but it will be delicious regardless.) Strain out the solids and add the lime juice and salt. Store the finished tepache in an airtight container in the refrigerator, where it will keep 2 weeks.

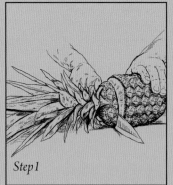

Step 1

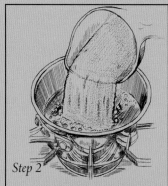

Step 2

Step 3

Step 4

Step 5

FERMENTATION FAILS

Anytime you're fermenting food, there's a risk of spoilage. Don't worry, though! With the three-days-max timeline, it's *extremely* unlikely this tepache will go awry. That said, if it does, you'll know. Millennia of evolution have programmed the human body to understand when food has gone bad. If this happens, throw it out and start over.

TEPACHE COLADA

GLASS: PINT

ICE: CRUSHED OR PEBBLE

1 ounce / 30 ml white rum

1 ounce / 30 ml rhum agricole

1 ounce / 30 ml cream of coconut

½ ounce / 15 ml tepache

Scant ½ ounce / 13 ml strained lime juice

Garnish: Grated cinnamon

Combine the ingredients with ice in a Boston shaker and vigorously shake for 20 seconds. Pack the glass with the ice. Strain the cocktail into the glass. Top with more crushed ice if needed. Garnish with grated cinnamon and serve.

TRY TEPACHE IN THESE OTHER COCKTAILS:

GIMLET (page 42): Replace half the lime juice with tepache.

RUNNING MATES (page 128): Replace the orange and lime juices with tepache.

WHISKEY SOUR (page 76): Remove the sugar and replace half the lemon juice with tepache.

BATANGA

1 lime

1½ ounces / 45 ml blanco tequila

Mexican Coca-Cola to top, about 4 ounces / 120 ml

Garnish: Kosher salt rim

Cut the lime in half with a medium kitchen knife (do not rinse the knife). Juice and strain the lime, then measure out and reserve ½ ounce/15 ml. Rim the glass with the salt and fill it with the ice. Add the reserved lime juice and the tequila. Top with Mexican Coke, stir the cocktail with the knife, and serve.

If you've been reading any of these introductions, it should be pretty obvious by now that cocktail history is cloudy, competitive, prone to mythmaking, and dependent on sometimes century-old receipts very few folks have kept. But there are some absolute people and places—like Harry's Bar in Venice, where the Bellini was invented, and the bar at Raffles in Singapore, birthplace of the Singapore Sling—that create something of a globe-crossing map for cocktail pilgrims.

Tequila (the town) is the ancestral seat of tequila (the spirit) in the Mexican state of Jalisco, 45 minutes outside Guadalajara. It boasts one of these essential stops, El Capilla, a humble cantina with lazily turning ceiling fans and walls decked with trophies and photos of the bar's capo, Don Javier Delgado Corona, creator of a simple but beloved cocktail called the Batanga sometime in the 1950s or '60s. (The most oft-mentioned date is 1961.) The drink is greater than the sum of its parts: blanco tequila, lime, salt, and Mexican Coca-Cola. It's a speedy and effective thirst-buster, the cane-sugar Coke fizzing and snapping like Pop Rocks in a tall glass, but some say the X factor is in the long, wood-handled knife Delgado Corona uses to stir the Batanga together. A magic wand for a magic cocktail.

BATANGA EXPRESS

In the mid-1990s, Pepsi released the coffee-soda experiment Pepsi Kona upon an unsuspecting Philadelphia test market. Maybe it was the taste, maybe it was the "Spank your senses" TV-spot tagline, but the drink bombed in less than a year, disappearing into bottled-beverage lore. There is something appealing about combining coffee and cola, though, and not just the double kick of caffeine. The bitterness of the former downplays the sweetness of the latter in a way that, in a cocktail, really works. That's what happens in the Batanga Express, basically a classic Batanga with a shot of espresso, lemon instead of lime, and a couple dashes of bitters.

1 lemon

1½ ounces / 45 ml blanco tequila

1 ounce / 30 ml brewed espresso, cooled

2 dashes Angostura bitters

Mexican Coca-Cola to top, about 3 ounces / 90 ml

Garnish: Kosher salt rim, expressed lemon peel

Cut the lemon in half with a medium kitchen knife (do not rinse the knife). Juice and strain the lemon, then measure out and reserve ½ ounce/15 ml. Rim the glass with the salt and fill it with the ice. Add the reserved lemon juice, the tequila, the espresso, and the bitters. Top with Mexican Coke and stir the cocktail with the knife. Garnish with the expressed lemon peel and serve.

EL CAPILLA

MAKES 1 COCKTAIL

GLASS: ROCKS | ICE: JUMBO CUBE

Named for Batanga padre Don Javier Delgado Corona's bar in Tequila, Jalisco, El Capilla uses silky homemade Lime Cordial in lieu of fresh lime juice. It's the first step in turning a snappy, kinetic crusher into a suave, cerebral sipper. Aged tequila builds in a backbone of oak, while the bittersweetness and rich spices of Bénédictine and Averna conjure a thinking person's cola. We like El Capilla shaken, but it would taste great as a stirred cocktail as well.

2 ounces / 60 ml reposado tequila

¾ ounce / 22 ml Averna amaro

½ ounce / 15 ml Bénédictine

½ ounce / 15 ml Lime Cordial

Garnish: Kosher salt rim, expressed lime peel

Rim one side of the glass with the salt and add the ice. Combine the ingredients in a Boston shaker and vigorously shake for 15 seconds. Strain the cocktail into the glass. Garnish with the expressed lime peel and serve.

LIME CORDIAL

MAKES ABOUT 1 CUP / 266 ML

3 ounces / 90 ml vodka

3 ounces / 90 ml strained lime juice

3 ounces / 90 ml Simple Syrup (page 4)

Combine the ingredients in an airtight container, vigorously shake, and store in the refrigerator, where it will keep for 1 month.

◀ Batanga Express, El Capilla, Batanga Tropica

BATANGA TROPICA

MAKES 1 COCKTAIL

GLASS: MEXICAN CLAY MUG | ICE: CRUSHED OR PEBBLE

Roughly 1,900 miles of indigo sea stretch between the Caribbean coast of the Yucatán Peninsula and the western shore of Barbados. This Batanga cuts the distance to zero by mixing tequila and Velvet Falernum, a Barbadian rum-based liqueur flavored with almond, cloves, and lime. (Other bottles labeled as only "falernum" are nonalcoholic syrups; John D. Taylor's, which contains booze, is the quintessential brand and the stuff you want here.) With pineapple and lime juices, cola syrup steeped with fresh mint, and plenty of crushed ice to round out the case, this is the Batanga squarely in tiki territory.

2 ounces / 60 ml añejo tequila

1½ ounces / 45 ml strained pineapple juice

1 ounce / 30 ml John D. Taylor's Velvet Falernum

¾ ounce / 22 ml Mint-Cola Syrup

½ ounce / 15 ml strained lime juice

Garnish: Spearmint sprig x 3, pineapple wedge

Combine the ingredients in a Boston shaker and vigorously shake for 20 seconds. Pack the mug with the ice. Strain the cocktail over the ice, garnish with the mint and pineapple, and serve.

MINT-COLA SYRUP

MAKES ABOUT 2 CUPS / 470 ML

1½ cups / 350 ml cola

1 cup / 200 g granulated sugar

20 large spearmint leaves

Combine the ingredients in a saucepot and simmer over medium heat, stirring to dissolve the sugar. Allow the mixture to cool to room temperature and strain off the mint. Transfer to an airtight container and store in the fridge, where it will keep for 2 weeks.

WORKSHOP:
YEAST-CARBONATED SODA

At restaurants and bars, blending syrup with carbonated water is typically how soda gets its bubbles. The low-fi version is to simply stir the still and sparkling components together by hand, while high-volume joints are more likely to rely on a soda gun or fountain, in which cola, lemon-lime, and other concentrates travel through a network of tubes and unite with seltzer in a pressurized gush, mixing as it fills your glass. Either way is dependent on carbonated water, something that wasn't commercially available before the mid-1700s. So how did people make bubbling beverages that didn't come from some freshwater forest spring back in the day?

Yeast. Yeast eats sugar. This produces alcohol and carbon dioxide (bubbles) that build up inside a contained environment (bottle). While sodas as we know them didn't exist in ancient times, people were certainly mixing water with fruit, honey, and vinegar syrups, and it's reasonable to assume strains of airborne wild yeast spawning natural carbonation was a fairly common phenomenon. Purposely yeasted sodas, however, are a mostly modern trend, often attributed to the home-brewing community.

The process is very easy: Just combine homemade syrup—kola for this workshop, to go with the Batanga—with water and a bit of Champagne yeast in a plastic soda bottle and wait. When the bottle feels rock-solid, enough carbon dioxide has built up, and the soda is carbonated. You won't get the explosive fizz of a force-carbonated soft drink, but more of a leisurely effervescence akin to sparkling water. This recipe works with any syrup you like, including the ones in this book like Makrut Lime Leaf (page 37), Apricot (page 75), and Chamomile Syrups (page 193), just make sure to add lemon or lime juice to balance the sweetness with acidity to taste.

MAKES 1 QUART / 1 L

½ batch Oleo-Saccharum (page 47) made from 2 lemons, 2 limes, 1 orange, and 2 lbs. / 0.9 kg demerara sugar

1 quart / 1 L water

4 tablespoons kola nut

3 cinnamon sticks, cracked

2 tablespoons dried bitter orange peel

2 teaspoons coriander seed

¼ teaspoon grated nutmeg

½ teaspoon vanilla extract

3½ cups / 830 ml spring or distilled water

¼ teaspoon Champagne yeast

Equipment: Vegetable peeler, medium pot, fine-mesh strainer, saucepot, 1 quart/1 L airtight container, 1 quart/ 1 L plastic soda bottle

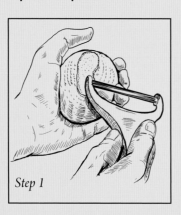

Step 1

Prepare the oleo-saccharum, being sure to reserve the citrus juices for later in the recipe. Then make the spice extract. Bring the water to a boil in a medium pot, add the kola nut, cinnamon, bitter orange peel, coriander, nutmeg, and vanilla and continue to boil for 10 minutes. Reduce the heat to low and simmer the mixture for 30 minutes. Remove the pot from the heat and allow it to cool for 30 minutes, then strain the liquid through a fine-mesh strainer and add it back to the saucepot. Bring the spice extract to a low boil and add the oleo-saccharum, gently stirring to completely dissolve. Remove the pot from the heat and allow it to cool for 30 minutes, then stir in the reserved citrus juices. Strain the mixture through a fine-mesh strainer and measure out and reserve 4 ounces/ 120 ml. Transfer the remaining syrup to an airtight container, where it will keep in the refrigerator for 2 weeks.

Fill the bottle with the reserved syrup and water and top with the yeast. Screw on the cap and shake to mix the ingredients. Set the bottle in a cool, dark place for 24 to 48 hours. As the yeast carbonates the liquid, the pressure will build against the bottle. When the bottle feels very hard, move it to the fridge to pause the carbonation. Chill for at least 2 hours before serving and open carefully.

Step 2

Step 3

Step 4

Step 5

Step 6

Step 7

NAKED AND FAMOUS

MAKES 1 COCKTAIL
GLASS: COUPE | ICE: NONE

¾ ounce / 22 ml joven mezcal

¾ ounce / 22 ml Aperol

¾ ounce / 22 ml yellow
Chartreuse

¾ ounce / 22 ml strained
lime juice

Garnish: Lime slice

Chill the glass. Combine the ingredients in a Boston shaker with ice and vigorously shake for 30 seconds. Strain the cocktail into the glass, garnish with the lime, and serve.

Not all classic cocktails are 100 years old. In the case of the Naked and Famous, well, it's not even old enough to legally drink. A bartender named Joaquín Simó created the Naked and Famous in 2011 while working at the influential New York bar Death & Co. and has famously described the cocktail as "the bastard love child of a classic Last Word and a Paper Plane, conceived in the mountains of Oaxaca." In the ensuing years, it's become a respected addition to contemporary bartending canon, and one of the few that put mezcal in a starring role.

Before getting to know the Naked and Famous, you should know its parents. There's a real age difference between them. The Last Word (gin, absinthe, green Chartreuse, Maraschino, lime) dates all the way back to Prohibition, while the Paper Plane (Bourbon, Aperol, Nonino, lemon) is considered another modern classic from post-2000 NYC bartending circles. Simó took the Chartreuse and lime from the former, the Aperol from the latter, and subbed in mezcal as the base spirit. The resulting cocktail is smoky, tart, botanical, and refreshing. This recipe calls for a joven ("young") mezcal, which is the mezcal analogue to blanco tequila. Brands we like include Ilegal, Vicio, and Montelobos.

MEZCAL AND TEQUILA— WHAT'S THE DIFFERENCE?

While both spirits are made from the piñas of the agave plant, tequila is made exclusively from the *blue* agave. Mezcal, meanwhile, can be made from many, many other species. Another point of differentiation lies in the production: When making tequila, the piñas get steamed in an oven, while mezcal's piñas are roasted in an earthen pit, creating the common top-note of smokiness often associated with mezcal.

BODY ELECTRIC

This easy evolution of the Naked and Famous spins the cocktail into a Spritz (page 100) format. The measure of mezcal remains the same as in the classic, while the Aperol, Chartreuse, and lime make room for a festive cascade of sparkling wine.

¾ ounce / 22 ml joven mezcal

½ ounce / 15 ml Aperol

½ ounce / 15 ml yellow Chartreuse

½ ounce / 15 ml strained lime juice

4 ounces / 120 ml prosecco or cava

Garnish: Lime wheel x 3

Set up the glass with the ice. Add the mezcal, Aperol, Chartreuse, and lime juice in the glass and briskly stir with a barspoon to incorporate. Top with the wine and stir for 5 seconds. Tuck the limes into the glass and serve.

BARE ESSENTIALS

MAKES 1 COCKTAIL
GLASS: ROCKS | ICE: CRUSHED OR PEBBLE

In the Bare Essentials, the Naked and Famous quartet loses one member, Aperol. Luxardo Bitter, an amaro with strong flavors of bitter orange and woody herbs, steps in to join the usual mezcal, Chartreuse, and citrus juice. Meanwhile, homemade chamomile syrup adds sweetness and a musky, honeyed-floral character that is absolutely dynamite with agave-based spirits. Try a dose in a Margarita (page 164).

1 ounce / 30 ml joven mezcal
¾ ounce / 22 ml yellow Chartreuse
¾ ounce / 22 ml strained lemon juice
½ ounce / 15 ml Luxardo Bitter Bianco
½ ounce / 15 ml Chamomile Syrup
Garnish: Lemon slice

Combine the ingredients in a Boston shaker with ice and vigorously shake for 20 seconds. Pack the glass with the ice. Strain the cocktail over the ice and mound more ice on top. Garnish with the lemon and serve.

CHAMOMILE SYRUP

MAKES ABOUT 2 CUPS / 470 ML

1 cup / 236 ml water

¼ cup plus 1 tablespoon / 10 g dried chamomile, or 8-10 chamomile tea bags

1 cup / 200 g granulated sugar

In a small saucepot on the stove, bring the water to a boil and add the chamomile. Turn off the heat, cover the pot, and let it steep for 5 minutes. Strain out and discard the blossoms and return the tea to the saucepot over medium-low heat. Add the sugar, stirring to completely dissolve. Remove the pot from the heat and allow it to completely cool. Transfer the finished chamomile syrup to an airtight container and store in the refrigerator, where it will keep for 2 weeks.

◀ Body Electric, Bare Essentials, Skin Contact

SKIN CONTACT

GLASS: ROCKS | ICE: SPHERE

The Skin Contact alters and amplifies the citrus component of the Naked and Famous by infusing mezcal with Buddha's hand, the claw-shaped fruit whose spindly fingers have a sweet lemon-blossom perfume. If you can't find Buddha's hand, this recipe will also work with regular or Meyer lemons, tangerines, and oranges. Try a mix to achieve an interesting citrus profile.

¾ ounce / 22 ml Buddha's Hand-Infused Reposado Mezcal

¾ ounce / 22 ml Select aperitivo

¾ ounce / 22 ml yellow Chartreuse

¾ ounce / 22 ml strained lime juice

Set up the glass with the ice. Combine ingredients in a Boston shaker with ice and vigorously shake for 20 seconds. Strain the cocktail into the glass and serve.

BUDDHA'S HAND-INFUSED REPOSADO MEZCAL

MAKES ABOUT 1½ CUPS / 350 ML

1½ cups / 350 ml reposado mezcal

1 cup diced Buddha's-hand citron

Dice the citron and measure off one cup. Combine the ingredients in an airtight container and allow to infuse for 2 days. Strain out the citron, pressing as much liquid out of it as possible. Add any pressed liquid back to the mezcal. Strain the mezcal into a clean airtight container to remove any leftover debris. This will keep indefinitely, but the citron flavor will begin to degrade after 1 month.

WORKSHOP:
FLAMING GARNISHES

Torched and scorched flora, flaming floats, alight oils—no doubt about it, pyrotechnics make cocktails look cool. But as much as these service techniques are about visual drama, they also make drinks more multidimensional by profoundly engaging your sense of smell. (Just imagine the aroma of smoldering cinnamon smoke twisting over a slug of whiskey.) In this workshop, a burst of burnt orange gives a savory citrus edge to the Naked and Famous, but the method can be applied to many different drinks. We've included a few other fiery tricks as well. Whichever you choose, just be sure to exercise caution and have a fire extinguisher nearby.

Equipment: Butane lighter; matches; fire extinguisher (Just in case!)

FLAMED ORANGE PEEL

Naked and Famous or desired cocktail

1 orange

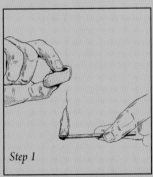

Step 1

Step 2

Cut a rectangular peel about 1 inch by 2 inches/2.5 cm by 5 cm. Hold the peel between your index finger and thumb with the skin side down, over the surface of your cocktail. With your other hand, ignite a lighter or match and position the flame between the orange peel and the drink. Quickly pinch the peel, so the expressed oils hit the flame and the resulting sparks land on top of the drink. Run the peel around the rim of the glass, drop it into the drink, and serve.

WORKS WELL WITH:
STIFF COCKTAILS
CORPSE REVIVER NO. 1 (page 58)
MANHATTAN (page 84)
NEGRONI (page 50)

FLOAT

Desired cocktail
Overproof spirit or liqueur,
such as Bacardi 151 rum

Step 1

Step 2

Place a barspoon upside down as close as possible to the surface of the drink. Gently pour a small amount of the spirit or liqueur down the back curve of the spoon; it will "float" on the surface of the drink. Using the lighter, carefully light the float on fire. Blow out before drinking.

WORKS WELL WITH:

TIKI AND TROPICAL COCKTAILS
MANGO MAI TAI (page 151)
PIÑA COLADA (page 174)
RUNNING MATES (page 128)

CINNAMON IGNITION

Desired cocktail

Ground cinnamon

Step 1

Follow the instructions for the Float. Once the surface of the cocktail is alight, sprinkle the cinnamon into the flames for a sparkle effect. This works with other ground spices, too.

WORKS WELL WITH:

SPICED COCKTAILS
BRANDY ALEXANDER FLIP (page 161)
PIÑA COQUITO (page 178),
SANDERSON SISTER (page 62)

Step 2

Step 3

ROSEMARY/CINNAMON INCENSE

Desired cocktail

1 rosemary sprig or 1 cinnamon stick

WORKS WELL WITH:
WHISKEY COCKTAILS
BREAKFAST MANHATTAN, REVERSED
(page 88)
OLD FASHIONED (page 68)
WHISKEY SOUR (page 76)

Place the "incense" in the cocktail as you would a straw and using the lighter, carefully light the exposed end on fire. Alternately, lay it across the rim of the glass and light the top of the rosemary or either side of the cinnamon. It will begin to smolder and smoke. Blow out before drinking.

NAKED AND FAMOUS

Step 1

Step 2

Step 3

WORKS CITED

AQUAFABA

Goldberg, Elyssa. "Everything You Need to Know About Aquafaba, the Vegan Wonder Ingredient." *Bon Appetit*. Condé Nast. May 10, 2016. https://www.bonappetit.com/test-kitchen/ingredients/article/aquafaba-health-benefits.

BRANDY ALEXANDER

Difford, Simon. "Alexander cocktail." Difford's Guide. Odd Firm of Sin Ltd. https://www.diffordsguide.com/encyclopedia/1072/cocktails/alexander-cocktail.

CORPSE REVIVER

Author unknown. *Punch, Or the London Charivari*. December 21, 1861. https://digi.ub.uni-heidelberg.de/diglit/punch1861a/0259/.

EL PRESIDENTE

Allan, M. Carrie. "This influential Cuban bartender wants to preserve the elegant tradition of the island's cantineros." *Washington Post*. May 24, 2019. https://www.washingtonpost.com/lifestyle/food/this-influential-cuban-bartender-wants-to-preserve-the-elegant-tradition-of-the-islands-cantineros/2019/05/23/4ce24dec-7cb1-11e9-8ede-f4abf521ef17_story.html.

Wondrich, David. "History Lesson: El Presidente Cocktail." *Imbibe*. November 6, 2012.

Yoon, Basil. *When It's Cocktail Time in Cuba*. New York: Horace Liveright, 1928.

FRENCH 75

Craddock, Harry. *The Savoy Cocktail Book*. London: Constable & Company, Ltd., 1930. https://euvs-vintage-cocktail-books.cld.bz/1930-The-Savoy-Cocktail-Book/72/.

Judge Jr. *Here's How!* New York: Leslie-Judge Company, 1927. https://euvs-vintage-cocktail-books.cld.bz/1927-Here-s-How-2nd-impression/28.

Simonson, Robert. "In Search of the Ultimate French 75." *Punch*. Penguin Random House. December 13, 2018. https://punchdrink.com/articles/ultimate-best-french-75-cocktail-recipe/.

Wondrich, David. "Behind the Drink: The French 75." Liquor.com. Dotdash. Date unknown. https://www.liquor.com/articles/behind-the-drink-the-french-75/.

GIMLET

Baker, Charles H. *The Gentleman's Companion—Vol. II Exotic Drinking Book*. New York: The Derrydale Press, 1939.

GRASSHOPPER

DeJesus, Erin. "It's Not Easy Being Green: The Weird History of The Grasshopper." Eater. Vox. October 23, 2014. https://www.eater.com/2014/10/23/7036159/a-brief-history-of-the-grasshopper https://euvs-vintage-cocktail-books.cld.bz/1862-The-bar-tenders-guide-1862-2-50/142.

JULEP

Bullock, Tom. *The Ideal Bartender*. Self-published: 1917. https://euvs-vintage-cocktail-books.cld. bz/1917-The-Ideal-Bartender-by-Tom-Bullock/42/.

Davis, John. *Travels of Four Years and a Half in the United States of America*. Library of Congress. https:// cdn.loc.gov/service/gdc/lhbtn/24800/24800.pdf.

Moskowitz, Brett. "Mint Condition: What you never knew about the mint julep." Tasting Table. May 5, 2017. https://www.tastingtable.com/drinks/national/mint-julep-history-derby-day.

MANHATTAN

Wondrich, David. "The Strangely Cool Origin Story of the Manhattan." The Daily Beast. IAC. July 13, 2017. https://www.thedailybeast.com/the-strangely-cool-origin-story-of-the-manhattan.

MARGARITA

Difford, Simon. "Margarita cocktail." Difford's Guide. Odd Firm of Sin, Ltd. https://www.diffordsguide. com/g/1138/margarita-cocktail/origins-and-history.

MAI TAI

Bergeron, Victor J. *Trader Vic's Bartender's Guide*. New York: Doubleday & Company, Inc., 1972.

MARTINI

Wondrich, David. "The Coming of the Martini: An Annotated Timeline." The Daily Beast. IAC. March 30, 2018. https://www.thedailybeast.com/the-coming-of-the-martini-an-annotated-timeline.

OLD FASHIONED

Difford, Simon, and Robert Simonson. "Old Fashioned cocktail." Difford's Guide. Odd Firm of Sin Ltd. https://www.diffordsguide.com/encyclopedia/500/cocktails/old-fashioned-cocktail.

PIÑA COLADA

Candee, Marjorie Dent. "Gourmet's Guide Along the Old Spanish Main: At the Bar." *New York Times*. April 16, 1950. https://timesmachine.nytimes.com/timesmachine/1950/04/16/132813902. html?pageNumber=271.

OLEO

Jones, Carey, and John McCarthy. "Up the Citrus in Your Cocktails with Oleo Saccharum." *Saveur*. February 16, 2016. https://www.saveur.com/how-to-make-oleo-saccharum/.

SPRITZ

Baiocchi, Talia, and Leslie Pariseau. *Spritz*. Berkeley: Ten Speed Press, 2016. https://www.amazon.com/ Spritz-Italys-Aperitivo-Cocktail-Recipes/dp/1607748851.

INDEX